Aleene's Joy of Giving

Aleene and Heidi

Oxmoor House

Aleene's® Joy of Giving
from the Best of ALEENE'S CREATIVE LIVING® Series
©1999 by Oxmoor House, Inc.
Book Division of Southern Progress Corporation
P.O. Box 2463, Birmingham, Alabama 35201

Published by Oxmoor House, Inc., and Leisure Arts, Inc.

Library of Congress Catalog Card Number: 98-68395
Hardcover ISBN: 0-8487-1877-1
Softcover ISBN: 0-8487-1878-X
Manufactured in the United States of America
First Printing 1999

Designs by Heidi Borchers

Editor-in-Chief: Nancy Fitzpatrick Wyatt
Senior Crafts Editor: Susan Ramey Cleveland
Senior Editor, Copy and Homes: Olivia Kindig Wells
Art Director: James Boone

Aleene's® Joy of Giving
Editor: Catherine Corbett Fowler
Copy Editor: L. Amanda Owens
Senior Photographer: John O'Hagan
Photo Stylist: Linda Baltzell Wright
Illustrator: Kelly Davis
Contributing Designer: Carol Damsky
Senior Production Designer: Larry Hunter
Publishing Systems Administrator: Rick Tucker
Director, Production and Distribution: Phillip Lee
Associate Production Manager: Theresa L. Beste
Production Assistant: Faye Porter Bonner

Aleene's® is a federally registered trademark of Artis, Inc.
Trademark Registration #1504878
Aleene's® is used by permission of Artis, Inc.

Cover portrait of Aleene Jackson and Heidi Borchers by Craig Cook

We're Here for You!
We at Oxmoor House are dedicated to serving you with reliable information that expands your imagination and enriches your life. We welcome your comments and suggestions. Please write us at:

Oxmoor House, Inc.
Editor, *Aleene's Joy of Giving*
2100 Lakeshore Drive
Birmingham, AL 35209

To order additional publications, call
1-205-877-6560.

Introduction

"It's better to give than to receive" is so true for me.

The pleasure I experience when I present a gift to a special person is unbeatable. And if the gift is something that I have made myself, the pleasure is doubled. Handmade items allow me to share a little bit of myself and my talent with the recipient. Additionally, I am able to personalize the gift; I can choose colors and motifs that I know will suit someone's personality. (And handcrafted presents are often less expensive than store-bought objects.)

With these thoughts in mind, I have designed more than 50 projects for a wide variety of gift-giving occasions. I have tried to create unique items that don't require a lot of time to make and that will appeal to a variety of tastes. (Remember, you want the gift to suit the tastes of the recipient, not necessarily your preferences.) So flip through the pages of suggestions in this book and start experiencing the *Joy of Giving*.

Heidi

Contents

Page 40

Page 59

Page 85

Personal Style 76

*Gifts to give her wardrobe and
    spirits a lift*

Everyday Pleasures 102

Tokens of affection to make any day special

Page 134

Holidays & Celebrations

Page 11

Page 26

Whatever the reason for celebrating, the gift ideas found in this chapter are sure to please. Handcrafted ornaments, cards, and more seasonal tributes show just how much you care. Remember, the best things in life are made with love.

Page 40

Heartfelt Valentines

Here are two thoughtful yet simple ways to express your feelings. Fill the heart-shaped envelope with flowers, candy, or maybe a gift certificate. Or add a little romance to a room by hanging a pretty stuffed felt heart or two from a doorknob.

❧ Materials ❧

For each: Pinking shears
Aleene's Tacky Glue™
Thread
For heart envelope: Felt: 2 (6" x 8") pieces red,
 1 (4½" x 5½") piece white, dark pink scrap
1 (26") length ⅛"-wide pink satin ribbon
Assorted Aleene's Botanical Preserved Flowers &
 Foliage™ (optional)
For each stuffed heart: Felt: 2 (6" x 8") pieces
 first color, 1 (4½" x 5½") piece second color,
 1 (3" x 4") piece third color
Embroidery needle and embroidery floss
Stuffing
Ribbons: 1 (16") length ⅛"-wide satin, 1 (18")
 length 1"-wide sheer

Directions for heart envelope

1 Transfer patterns on page 10 to felt and cut 2 large hearts from red and letters from dark pink. Using pinking shears, cut 1 medium heart from white.

2 Center and glue medium heart on 1 red heart for envelope front. Referring to photo for positioning, glue letters on white heart. Let dry.

3 With right side up and edges aligned, stack envelope front on remaining red heart. Beginning and ending at dots (see pattern) and using ¼" seam allowance, machine-stitch hearts together around bottom point to make envelope.

4 Cut 1 (16") length and 2 (5") lengths from ⅛"-wide pink satin ribbon. Glue 1 end of 16" ribbon length inside envelope at each top side. Tie each 5" ribbon in bow. Glue bows on heart front

(see photo). Let dry. If desired, arrange dried flowers in envelope.

Directions for stuffed heart

1 Transfer patterns on page 10 to felt and cut 2 large hearts from first color and 1 small heart from third color. Using pinking shears, cut 1 medium heart from second color.

2 Center and glue medium heart on 1 large heart for front. Let dry. Center and stitch small heart on medium heart with embroidery floss, using

straightstitching or blanket stitching. With right side up and edges aligned, stack front on remaining large heart. Using ¼" seam allowance, machine-stitch hearts together, leaving small opening. Stuff heart and slipstitch opening closed.

3 Glue 1 end of 16" ribbon length between felt layers at top of each lobe of heart. Tie sheer ribbon in bow and glue to front of heart at top. Let dry.

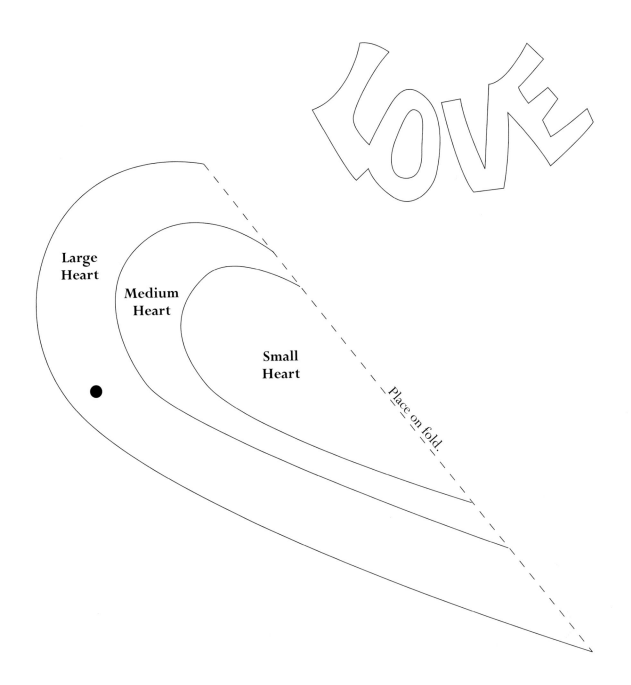

Large Heart

Medium Heart

Small Heart

Place on fold.

Love Notes

Remember the fun you had as a child cutting out paper hearts for that perfect Valentine? You can create that same magic today with these (slightly more grown-up) handmade cards.

❧ Materials ☙

For each: Aleene's Tacky Glue™

For flower card: 1 (6½" x 8¾") piece white card
stock

Paper: 1 (5" x 7") piece fuchsia, bright green and
yellow scraps

White paper plate with fluted edges

Red puff paint

For double-heart card: Paper: 1 (8" x 10") piece
light lavender paper; white, dark lavender, and
fuchsia scraps

Fun Foam scrap

Foam-core board

Sponge paintbrush

Aleene's Premium-Coat ™ Acrylic Paint: Dusty Violet

Aleene's 3-D Foiling™ Glue

Aleene's Gold Crafting Foil™

For gold heart card: Paper: 1 (5¾" x 6½") piece
dark lavender paper, white scrap

Gold ink pen

1 (3" x 4½") piece posterboard

2 (3" x 4½") pieces gold foil tissue paper

Directions for flower card

1 Fold card stock in half to make 4⅜" x 6½" card.
Tear edges of fuchsia paper so that it measures
approximately 3¾" x 6". Tear bright green paper scrap
so that it measures approximately ¼" x 3½". Cut ⅝"-
diameter circle from yellow paper scrap. Transfer
flower petal pattern to paper plate 9 times, positioning
pattern so that wide end of petal is over humps in flutes
of plate. Cut out flower petals.

2 Center torn fuchsia rectangle on front of card.
Glue in place. Referring to photo, glue bright
green stem, paper plate flower petals, and yellow
flower center to front of card. Let dry.

3 Use red puff paint to paint small hearts freehand on
card front. Let dry.

Directions for double-heart card

1 Fold light lavender paper in half so that it measures
5" x 8". Position card so that 5" edges are at top
and bottom. Using pencil, lightly draw line across width
of card, 5½" above bottom edge of card. Transfer small

heart to white scrap of paper 2 times and cut out
hearts. Referring to photo, position hearts on line
drawn across top of card. Lightly trace around hearts.
Remove hearts. Cutting through both layers of paper,
cut along marked pencil line and along outline of
hearts.

2 To make stamp, transfer swirl pattern to Fun Foam
and cut out. Glue foam swirl to scrap of foam-core
board. Dip paintbrush into Dusty Violet. Apply even
coat of paint to swirl stamp. Press stamp firmly onto
card front. Repeat to stamp additional swirls on card
front as desired. Let dry.

3 Transfer small heart pattern once to dark lavender
paper scrap and once to fuchsia paper scrap. Do not
cut out hearts. Apply very thin line of 3-D Foiling Glue
along edges of hearts. Let dry. (Glue will be opaque and
sticky when dry. Glue must be thoroughly dry before
foil is applied.) To apply gold foil, lay foil dull side down
on top of glue lines. Using finger, gently but firmly
press foil onto glue, completely covering glue with foil.
Peel away foil paper. Carefully tear hearts outside foil
line.

4 Referring to photo and marked lines, position
hearts on front of card and glue in place. Using
very thin line of 3-D Foiling Glue, write "Love" on
front of card. Let dry. Apply foil as in Step 3.

Directions for gold heart card

1 Fold dark lavender paper in half so that it measures
3½" x 5¾". Referring to photo and using gold ink
pen, repeatedly write "Love" diagonally across front of
card.

2 Coat front of posterboard piece with glue. Press
piece of gold tissue into glue, aligning edges.
Smooth out wrinkles. Repeat for opposite side of
posterboard piece. Let dry. Transfer large heart pattern
to tissue-covered posterboard piece. Cut out heart.

3 From white paper scrap, cut ¼" x 9" strip. Notch
each end of strip. Using gold ink pen, write "Love"
repeatedly along length of strip. Referring to photo,
fold white paper strip around gold heart. Glue strip in
place. Glue heart to center front of card.

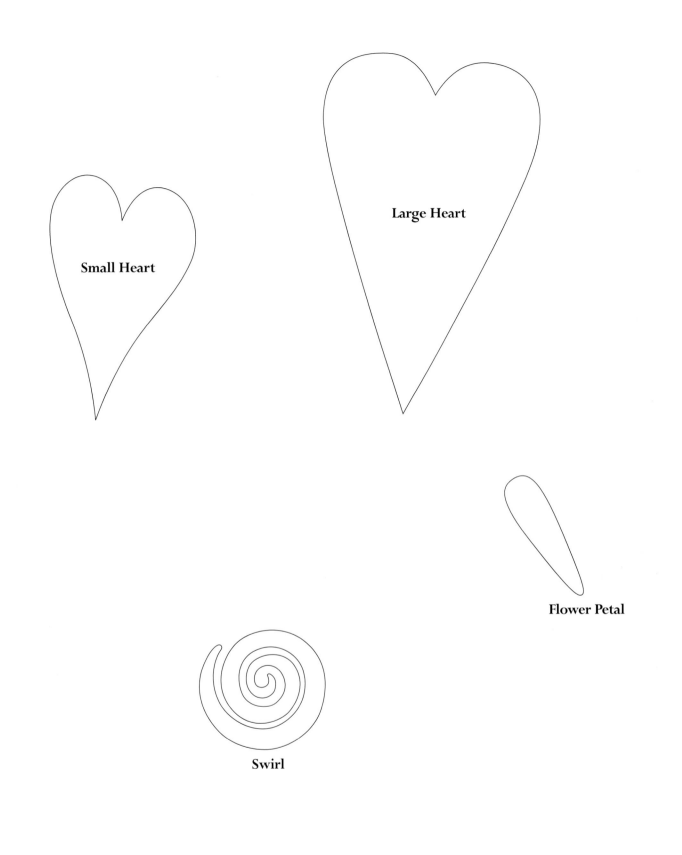

Small Heart

Large Heart

Flower Petal

Swirl

Easter Banner

Make this bright banner in less time than it takes to find the prize egg! The appliqués are fused in place and then outlined with dimensional paint for a truly quick-and-easy project.

❧ Materials ❧

Aleene's Fusible Web™
Fabrics: dark blue scraps for wording; 1 (18" x 30") piece green plaid; 1 (10" x 12") piece each purple, yellow, orange, and hot pink; 1 (6" x 9") piece each yellow print, light purple print, pink-and-white check, dark purple check, and hot pink print; 1 (29" x 43") piece light blue
White fabric marking pencil
2" alphabet stencils
Dimensional fabric paints: green, orange, purple, hot pink
1 (34") length ½"-diameter wooden dowel
Ribbons: 1½ yards for hanger, variety widths and lengths for streamers (optional)

Directions

1 Fuse web to wrong side of dark blue fabric scraps. Using fabric marking pencil and alphabet stencils, transfer "Happy Easter" to right side of dark blue scraps. Cut out fabric letters. Set aside.

2 Fuse web to wrong side of remaining fabrics. Transfer leaf pattern (on page 16) to right side of green plaid 4 times; reverse pattern and transfer 2 times. Transfer tulip pattern (on page 17) to right side of purple, yellow, orange, and hot pink 1 time each. Transfer egg pattern (on page 16) 1 time each to remaining appliqué fabrics. Cut out shapes. Remove paper backing from all cutout fabric pieces.

3 From fusible web, cut 2 (½" x 43") strips and 2 (½" x 29") strips. To hem side edges of banner, on wrong side, press 1 (½" x 43") fusible web strip along each long edge of light blue fabric piece. Remove paper backing. Fold each long edge ½" to wrong side and fuse in place. On wrong side, press 1 (½" x 29") fusible web strip along each short edge of light blue piece. Remove paper backing. To hem bottom of banner, fold bottom edge ½" to wrong side and fuse in place. For top casing, fold top edge 2¼" to wrong side and fuse in place.

4 Referring to photo, position appliqué pieces on banner background. From light blue fabric scraps, cut pieces to fit back areas of eggs that extend beyond edges of banner. Fuse appliqués in place, making sure light blue fabric pieces are positioned beneath egg extensions.

5 Referring to photo and using dimensional paints, outline leaves with wavy lines, add veins down center of leaves, and paint zigzag stem beneath each tulip with green; outline yellow egg with orange; outline light purple egg and dark purple egg with purple; and outline pink-and-white egg and hot pink egg with hot pink. Let dry.

6 Insert wooden dowel through casing. For hanger, tie 1 end of 1½ yard ribbon length to each end of dowel near banner. If desired, tie remaining ribbon lengths to each end of dowel for streamers.

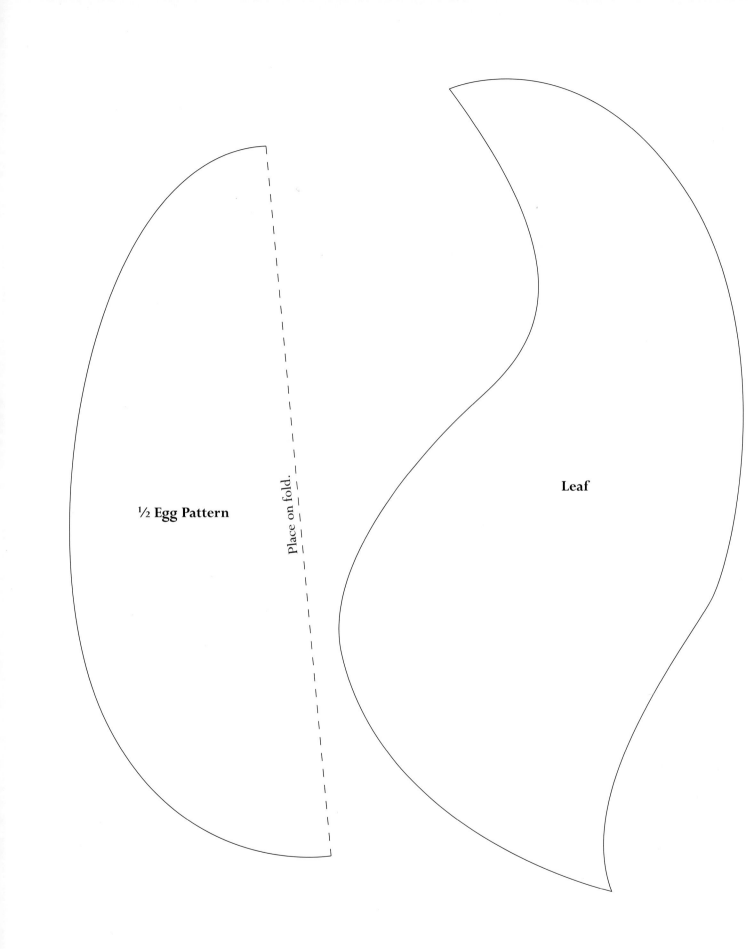

½ Egg Pattern

Place on fold.

Leaf

16

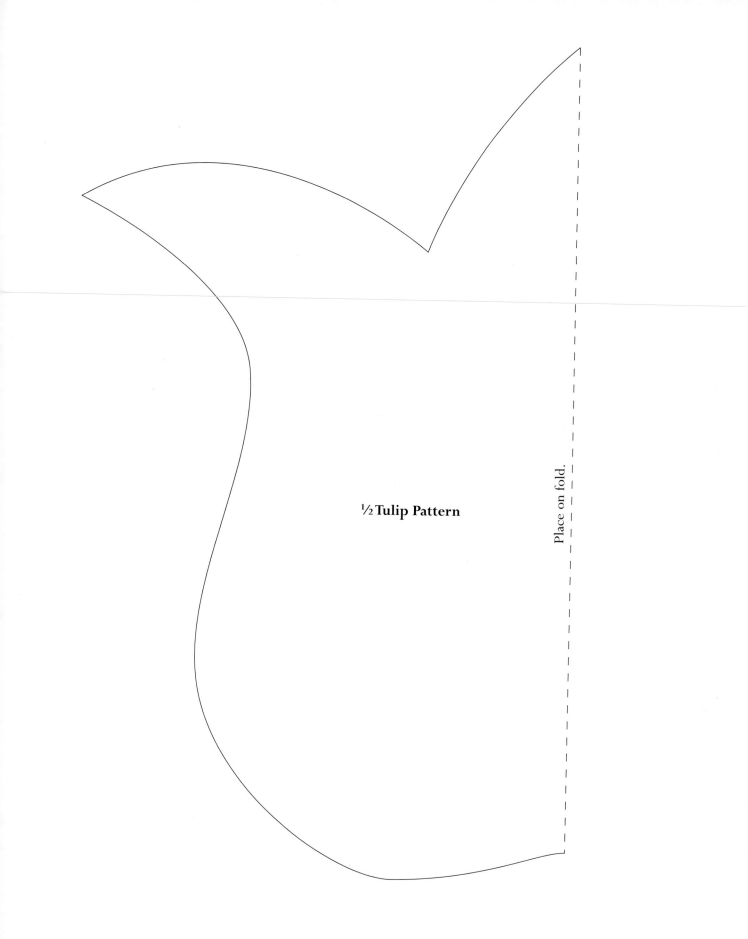

½ Tulip Pattern

Place on fold.

Cottontail Couple

Look who's hopping down the bunny trail! This dapper bunny couple,
made from clay pots, looks adorable decorating a hutch.

❧ Materials ☙
(for both bunnies)
6 (3½") clay pots
2 (4"-diameter) clay saucers
White spray paint
Aleene's Ultimate Glue Gun™
Aleene's All-Purpose Glue Sticks™
Fun Foam: white, pink
Lace: 1 (3") length 1⅜"-wide flat, 1(12") length ½"-wide flat, 1 (8") length 1¼"-wide pregathered
Fabric: 1 (3" x 18") strip and 2" square multi-colored checked; 1 (7½" x 12¼") piece and 1 (1½" x 12") strip denim
Needle and thread
1 (18") length ⅜"-wide light green ribbon
Purple ribbon rose
2 miniature straw baskets
Pom-poms: 4 (1½") white, 2 (⅜") black
Shank buttons: 2 (½") green, 2 (½") blue s
Small silk flowers
1 straw hat each for girl and boy
Craft knife

Directions

1 Spray-paint clay pots and saucers white. Let dry. Turn 1 saucer upside down. Referring to Diagram A, hot-glue 1 clay pot, right side up, to bottom of saucer. Turn second clay pot upside down and stack on first clay pot; glue rims together. Stack third clay pot, right side up, on top of second clay pot and hot-glue bottoms of pots together. Repeat with remaining pots and saucer.

2 **For each,** using patterns on page 20, transfer 1 outer ear pattern and 1 arm pattern to white Fun Foam; reverse patterns and transfer again. Then transfer 1 inner ear pattern to pink Fun Foam; reverse pattern and transfer again. Cut out shapes. Center and hot-glue 1 inner ear on top of each outer ear.

3 **For girl,** referring to photo, hot-glue 1⅜"-wide flat lace to center pot of 1 clay-pot bunny. For skirt, run gatherering thread along 1 long edge of 3" x 18" strip of checked fabric. Slightly fray opposite long edge of strip. Hot-glue gathered edge of skirt to bunny along rim of center pot. Overlap open ends of skirt at back and hot-glue together. Hot-glue ½"-wide lace along gathered edge of skirt and 1¼"-wide pregathered lace around bunny where bottoms of center and top pot are joined. Cut 8" length of light green ribbon and tie in bow. Referring to photo, hot-glue bow to front gathered edge of skirt. Hot-glue ribbon rose to neck of bunny.

4 **For boy,** to make overalls, trim 7½" x 12¼" piece as shown in Diagram B (on page 20). Cut 2" slit in center of bottom edge of overalls. Fold cut edges of slit to wrong side and hot-glue in place (see photo). Fold ½" of bottom edge under and hot-glue in place. Referring to photo, hot-glue overalls to remaining clay-pot bunny. For belt, fold long edges of 1½" x 12" denim strip under and hot-glue in place. Hot-glue belt around bunny along rim of center pot. Transfer pocket pattern to 2" square of checked fabric and cut out. Referring to photo, hot-glue sides and bottom of pocket to bib of overalls.

5 **For each,** referring to photo, hot-glue 2 arms to bunny; hot-glue 1 basket in hand. (Baskets may hold better glued to body rather than Fun Foam hand.) Referring to photo, hot-glue 2 white pom-poms to face for cheeks. For nose, hot-glue 1 black pom-pom on top of white pom-poms. Hot-glue 1 set of green or blue buttons in place for eyes.

6 **For girl,** hot-glue silk flowers around base of girl's straw hat. **For boy,** hot-glue remaining light green ribbon around base of boy's hat. **For each,** referring to photo, position 2 ears on hat and mark position with pencil. Using craft knife, slit through hat at marks. Slip ears through slits in hat. Hot-glue hat and ears to top of bunny.

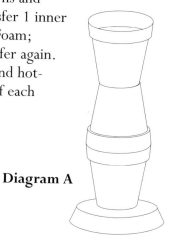

Diagram A

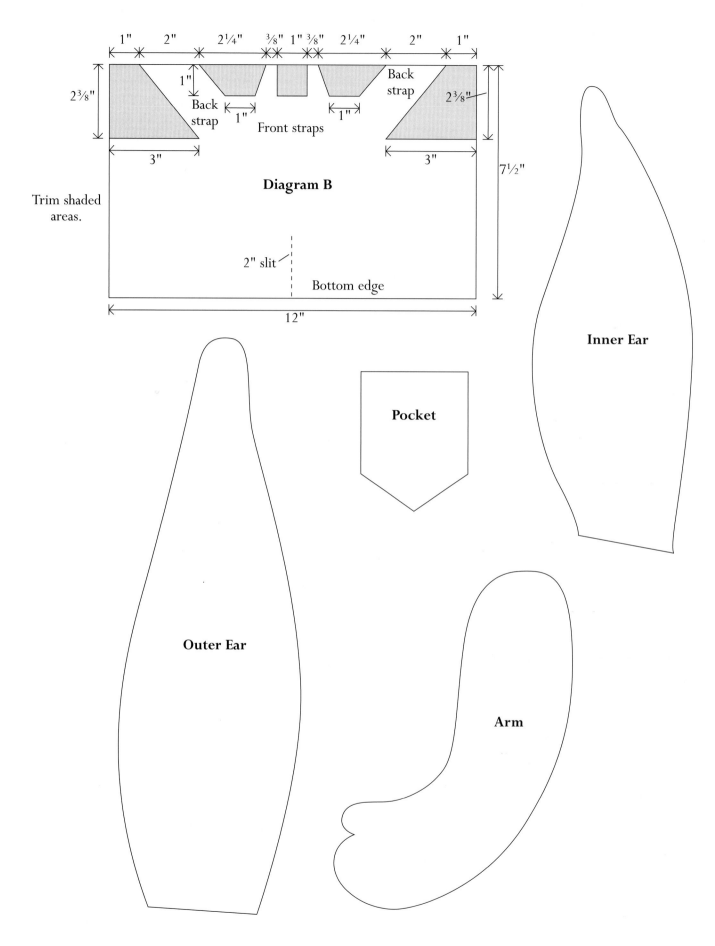

1"   2"   2¼"   ⅜" 1" ⅜"   2¼"   2"   1"

2³⁄₈"

1"

Back strap

1"

Front straps

1"

Back strap

Back strap

2³⁄₈"

3"

3"

Diagram B

Trim shaded areas.

7½"

2" slit

Bottom edge

12"

Inner Ear

Pocket

Outer Ear

Arm

Bridal Beauties

Lace, ribbons, pearls, and buttons decorate a bridal gift set that is both pretty and practical. The bride will find the card file box a great help in keeping track of wedding gifts and the thank-you notes she's written. And the picture mat will showcase her wedding portrait in grand style.

Directions for picture mat

1 Referring to tips below, fuse web to wrong side of lace. Fuse lace to right side of mat. Trim excess lace from picture opening, leaving 1" all around. Fold excess lace to back of mat and fuse, clipping curves as needed.

2 Tie ribbon in bow. Glue bow and assorted trims to mat as desired. Let dry.

Directions for box

1 Following BoxMaker directions, cut box blank to desired size for box and lid. Cut 1 piece of lace to cover right side of box and lid. Referring to tips below, fuse web to wrong side of each piece of lace. Fuse lace to right side of matching box piece.

2 Complete box, following BoxMaker directions. Tie ribbon in bow. Glue bow and assorted trims to box lid as desired. Let dry.

Crafting Tips

This picture mat and box require that you apply fusible web to lace, which could be a very messy operation if you don't plan ahead. Follow these steps to keep from getting fusible web on your iron and ironing board.

• Cover your ironing board with a piece of fusible web paper (without the web) or with a piece of smooth fabric that can be discarded afterward.

• Stack the lace (right side down) with a piece of fusible web (paper side up) on the protected ironing board.

• Fuse the web to the lace. Remove the release paper from the web.

• Stack the picture mat or box piece (right side up) and the lace (web side down) on the protected ironing board.

• Place another piece of fusible web paper (without the web) on top and fuse the lace to the project item.

☙ Materials ☙

For each: Aleene's Fusible Web™
Aleene's Designer Tacky Glue™
Assorted buttons, beads, pearls, and ribbon flowers
For picture mat: 1 piece ivory lace to cover mat front
Purchased ivory mat to fit desired frame
1 (22") length ½"-wide ivory ribbon
For box: Aleene's BoxMaker™ and BoxBlanks™
Ivory lace to cover box and lid
1 (20") length 1½"-wide ivory wire-edged ribbon
1 (18½") length ½"-wide ivory trim

Happy Graduation

Don't know what to give a grad? Tuck money inside one of these fun-to-make cards. Your favorite graduate is sure to love it!

❧ Materials ❧

(for each card)

1 (6½" x 8½") piece watercolor paper
Craft knife
Aleene's Tacky Glue™
Fine-tip permanent marker
Assorted colors Aleene's Premium-Coat™ Acrylic
   Paint
Paintbrushes: ¼" flat shader, fine-tip
Aleene's 3-D Foiling™ Glue
Aleene's Crafting Foil™: gold or silver

Directions

1 Transfer oval pattern to paper so that bottom of oval is about ¹¹⁄₁₆" from 1 short end and is centered along width of paper. Cut out oval, using craft knife. To form card, fold end of paper with oval cutout up 2¾" to form pocket. Glue side edges of pocket to secure, using Tacky Glue sparingly. Let dry. Draw scalloped border around oval cutout, using marker. Then fold top end of paper down over pocket.

2 Transfer desired pattern to card front (see photo). For each color of paint, mix 2 parts water with 1 part paint to make a thin wash. Paint design with thinned paint. Let dry.

3 Apply fine lines of 3-D Foiling Glue to card front to outline painted design and to add details. Let dry. (Glue will be opaque and sticky when dry. Glue must be thoroughly dry before foil is applied.) To apply foil, lay foil dull side down on top of glue lines. Using finger, press foil onto glue, completely covering glue with foil. Peel away foil paper.

4 Write desired message on card front, using marker.

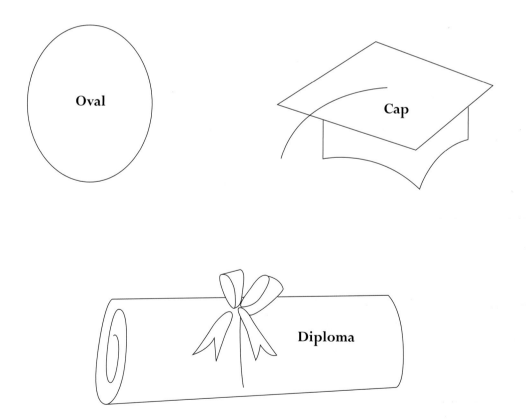

Oval

Cap

Diploma

Pumpkin Patch Pretties

For a happy Halloween treat, fill a gift basket with spiced cider mix, some ghost-shaped cookies, and a few soft-sculpture pumpkins. These gourds are a delightful fall accent for a den or a kitchen.

❧ Materials ❧
(for 1 pumpkin)
Needle and thread
Fabrics: 1 (10" x 24") orange print, 1 (1½" x 20") and
    1 (1½" x 10") strips in 2 different green prints
Stuffing
Aleene's Tacky Glue™
Upholstery needle and upholstery thread

Directions
1 Run gathering thread along each long edge of 10" x 24" fabric strip. Pull tightly to gather edges of fabric into circle and secure thread. Stuff pumpkin. Overlap ends of fabric and glue.

2 Thread upholstery needle with upholstery thread. Double thread and knot end. Insert needle into base of pumpkin at center. Push needle up through top center of pumpkin, take small stitch, and push needle back through to base of pumpkin, pulling fabric in at center. Repeat several times and tie off thread.

3 Tie 1½" x 20" strip of green fabric in bow. Notch ends of streamers. Tie 1½" x 10" strip of green fabric in knot around center knot of bow. Notch ends of 10" strip. Glue bow to center top of pumpkin.

Treat Sacks

Fuse fabric motifs to brown paper sacks to create these spirited gift bags.
They also make one-of-a-kind trick-or-treat sacks.

Materials
(for each sack)

Aleene's Fusible Web™
Print fabrics: assorted scraps, 1 (1¼" x 20") strip
2" alphabet stencils
Large paper sack with handles
Assorted colors dimensional paint
Fun Foam scrap
Aleene's Designer Tacky Glue™
Pencil with eraser
Aleene's Premium-Coat™ Acrylic Paint: True
    Yellow
Waxed paper

Directions

1 Fuse web to wrong side of fabric scraps. Transfer desired patterns to fabric scraps and cut out. Reverse desired stencils, transfer to remaining fabric scraps, and cut out. Referring to photo, fuse cutouts to paper sack. Embellish cutouts with dimensional paints (see photo). Let dry.

2 To make star stamp, transfer pattern to Fun Foam and cut 1 star. Glue star to pencil eraser. Let dry. Pour small puddle of True Yellow onto waxed paper. Dip star stamp into paint and press onto sack in desired position. Let dry.

3 Tie fabric strip in bow around handle of sack or tie bow and glue to sack. Let dry.

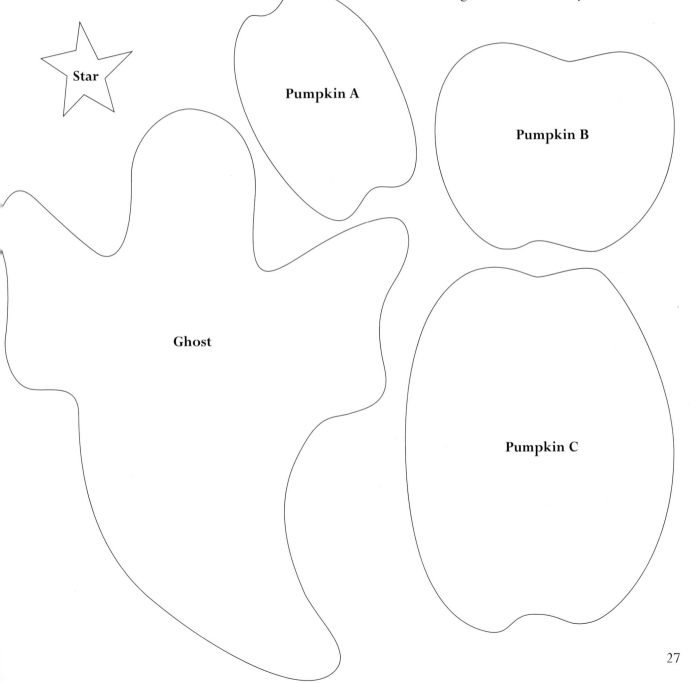

Star

Pumpkin A

Pumpkin B

Ghost

Pumpkin C

Turkey Day Banner

Thanksgiving guests will feel especially welcome when greeted by this festive banner. You'll be glad to know, it is entirely no-sew!

❧ Materials ❧

Aleene's Fusible Web™
1 (16½" x 17") piece natural batting
Felt: 1 (18") square brown; beige, brown, black, dark blue, off-white, gold, and red scraps
Brown print fabrics: 1 (7" x 9") piece each in 2 different prints, 1 (8") square, 2 (1½" x 15") torn strips
1⅜" alphabet stencils
Aleene's OK to Wash-It™ Glue
Small straw hat
2 (¼"-diameter) black half-round bead eyes
1 (18") length ⅜"-diameter wooden dowel
Copper spray paint
Brown embroidery floss

Directions

1 Fuse web to wrong side of batting. Center and fuse batting on brown felt square. Fuse web to wrong side of each 7" x 9" piece and to 8" square of brown fabric. Transfer patterns to 7" x 9" brown print fabrics and cut 3 feathers from each. Reverse letters, transfer to 8" brown print square, and cut 2 As, 2 Gs, 2 Hs, 2 Is, 1 K, 2 Ns, 2 Ps, 1 S, 1 T, 1 V, and 1 Y. Transfer patterns to felt and cut 1 body and 1 head from beige, 2 wings from brown, 1 feet from black, 1 coat from dark blue, 1 collar from off-white, 1 beak from gold, and 1 wattle from red.

2 Referring to photo, fuse feathers and letters in place on batting and glue felt pieces in place to form turkey. Let dry. Cut straw hat in half. Glue 1 hat half and bead eyes in place on turkey. (Set other hat half aside for another use.) Let dry.

3 For hanger loops, cut 2 (2" x 6¼") strips of brown felt. Fold each strip in half to form loop. Glue ends to back of banner, 2½" from each top corner. Let dry. Tie each brown fabric strip in bow. Glue 1 bow to banner at bottom of each hanger loop. Let dry.

4 Spray-paint dowel. Let dry. Slip dowel through hanger loops. Cut 1 (36") length of embroidery floss. Knot 1 end of floss at each end of dowel.

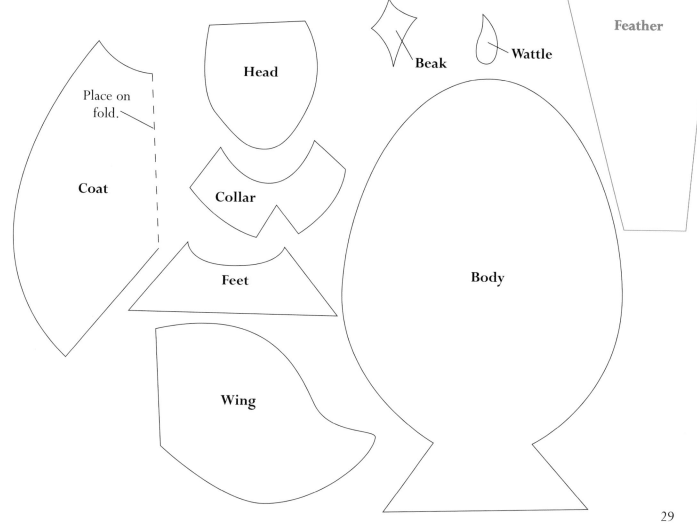

Head

Beak

Wattle

Feather

Place on fold.

Coat

Collar

Feet

Body

Wing

Scarecrow Vest

Embellish a purchased denim vest with fabric cutouts. To create an outfit, fuse additional motifs to a denim skirt.

❧ Materials ❧

Purchased denim vest
Assorted print fabric scraps
Aleene's Fusible Web™
Black dimensional paint
Aleene's Enhancers™ Textile Medium
Aleene's Premium-Coat™ Acrylic Paints: Burnt
    Umber, Dusty Beige, Deep Sage
Fine-tip paintbrush
Embroidery floss: brown, black
Assorted buttons
Aleene's OK to Wash-It™ Glue

Directions

1 Wash and dry vest and fabric scraps; do not use fabric softener in washer or dryer. Fuse web to wrong side of fabric scraps. Transfer patterns to fabrics and cut 2 heads, 2 hats, 2 shirts, 2 overalls,

4 straps, 2 small pumpkins, and 2 large pumpkins. From remaining fabrics, cut 5 small pieces for patches on scarecrows and 7 large odd-shaped pieces for patches on vest. Referring to photo, fuse fabric pieces in place on vest.

2 Paint facial features on each scarecrow with dimensional paint. Let dry. For each color of acrylic paint, mix equal parts textile medium and paint. Referring to photo, paint each scarecrow's post, grass, and vines and leaves on pumpkins, letting dry between colors. Paint ¼"-wide band around edges of vest and each armhole to look like binding. Let dry.

3 Referring to photo, stitch ⅜"- to 1"-long tufts of brown embroidery floss in place on each scarecrow for hair and straw. Add decorative straight-stitches to patches on vest with black embroidery floss. Glue 1 button to each patch. Let dry.

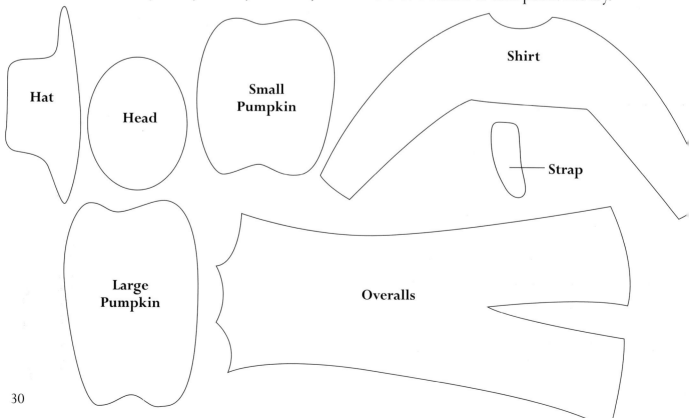

Hat

Head

Small Pumpkin

Shirt

Strap

Large Pumpkin

Overalls

31

Cozy Slippers

These slippers will warm her heart and toes! And she'll remember you fondly all winter long.

❧ Materials ❧

For each: 1 pair slippers with leather uppers
 (available in crafts and discount stores)
Aleene's Fusible Web™
For trees slippers: Green print fabric scrap
Aleene's Jewel-It™ Glue
6 (5-mm) crystal jewels
2 (9") lengths ⅛"-wide silver metallic ribbon
For snowflake slippers: Aleene's Enhancers™
 Textile Medium
Aleene's Premium-Coat™ Acrylic Paint: Deep
 Lavender
Paintbrush
White-on-white print fabric scrap
Silver dimensional paint

Directions

1 **For trees slippers,** fuse web to wrong side of green print fabric scrap. Transfer trees pattern to fabric and cut out appliqué for 1 slipper, trimming bottom of appliqué as needed to fit toe of slipper. Reverse pattern, transfer to fabric, and cut out appliqué for remaining slipper, trimming bottom of appliqué as needed to fit toe of slipper.

2 Fuse 1 appliqué on toe of each slipper. Glue 1 jewel at top of each tree on each slipper. Tie each ribbon in bow. Glue 1 bow to each slipper (see photo). Let dry.

3 **For snowflake slippers,** mix equal parts textile medium and paint. Paint leather portion of toe on each slipper Deep Lavender. Let dry. Fuse web to wrong side of white-on-white fabric. Transfer snowflake pattern to fabric and cut 2. Fuse 1 snowflake on toe of each slipper. Embellish toe of each slipper with dimensional paint as desired. Let dry.

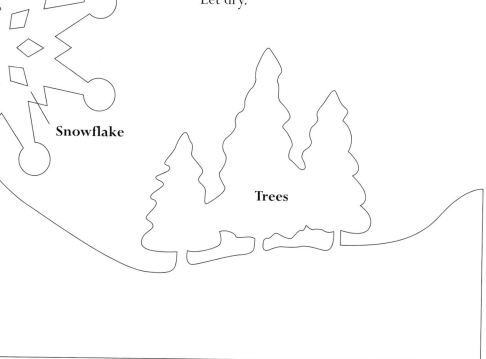

Snowflake

Trees

Star of David Suncatchers

Adorn a sunny window with these faux stained-glass suncatchers. They are beautiful reminders of a proud heritage on Jewish holidays—or any day of the year.

❧ Materials ❧

Aleene's Crafting Plastic™
Craft knife
Aleene's Tissue Paper™: white
Sponge paintbrush
Aleene's Paper Napkin Appliqué™ Glue
Aleene's 3-D Foiling™ Glue
Aleene's Crafting Foil™: gold or silver
Aleene's Premium Designer Brush™: shader
Aleene's Premium-Coat™ Acrylic Paints: True
    Lavender, Medium Yellow
⅛" hole punch
Jump rings
Assorted beads
Eye pins
Aleene's Satin Sheen Twisted Ribbon™: white
Suction cup hook

Directions for 1 star

1 Transfer desired star pattern on page 36 to crafting plastic and cut out, using craft knife. Cut 1 (8") square of tissue paper.

2 Using sponge brush, paint thin coat of Napkin Appliqué Glue onto 1 side of plastic star. Center star, glue side down, on top of tissue paper piece. Smooth tissue paper. Let dry. Using craft knife, trim excess tissue paper from edges of plastic star.

3 Center plastic star, tissue paper side down, on top of pattern. Using 3-D Foiling Glue, trace gray foil lines. Let dry. (Glue will be sticky when dry. Glue must be thoroughly dry before foil is applied.) To apply foil, lay foil dull side down on top of glue lines. Using your finger, press foil onto glue, completely covering glue with foil. Peel away foil paper.

4 Referring to photo and using shader brush, paint tissue paper side of star as shown, using True Lavender and Medium Yellow. Let dry.

5 Punch holes in 2 opposite points of star (see photo). Use jump rings, beads, and eye pins to embellish. (Make sure embellishment at top of star ends with jump ring.)

6 For hanger, tear twisted ribbon into strips. Holding several twisted ribbon strips as 1, tie strips in bow on jump ring. Attach suction cup hook to twisted ribbon bow to hang suncatcher on window.

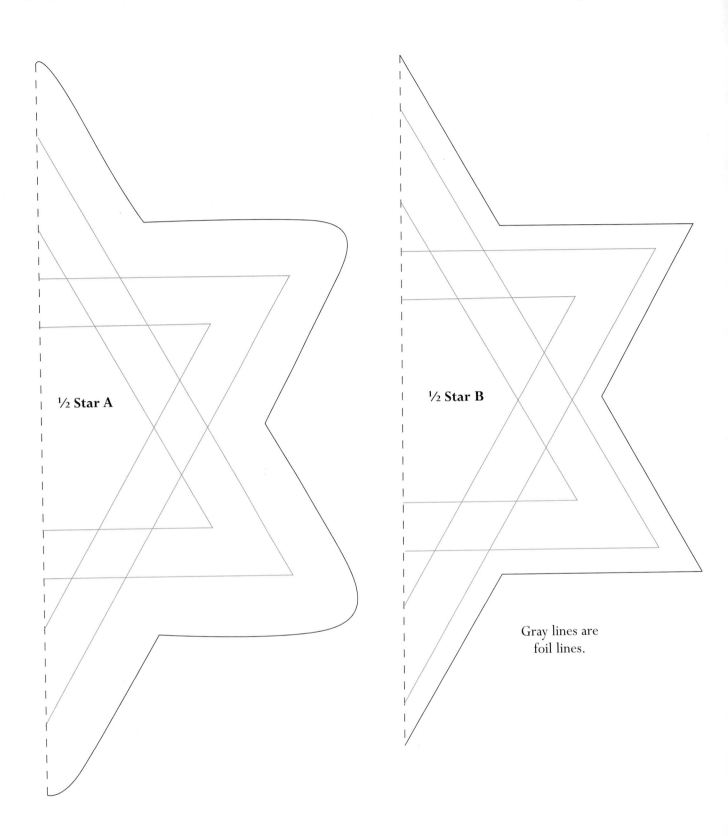

½ Star A

½ Star B

Gray lines are
foil lines.

Home Tweet Home

Nature-lovers will delight in these charming birdhouses. The bright colors make the ornaments stand out against evergreen branches.

This cute little bird is made from simply hot-gluing two red buttons together and adding a beak and a tail.

❧ Materials ❧

For each: Wire cutters or tin snips
Several large pinecones
Craft knife
Aleene's Ultimate Glue Gun™
Aleene's All-Purpose Glue Sticks™
Aleene's Premium-Coat™ Acrylic Paints: Deep
    Lavender, True Yellow, Burnt Umber, Black
Paintbrushes
Thin cardboard scrap
Assorted beads
Gold thread
Sheet moss
Assorted buttons with holes and shanks
Colored paper scraps
For blue birdhouse: Clean snack-sized raisin box
For red birdhouse: Clean and dry small juice can
Aleene's Premium-Coat™ Acrylic Paints: True Red,
    Deep Green
Small triangular sponge
20" length ¼" gold ribbon

Directions for blue birdhouse

1 Using cutters or snips, cut scales from pinecones. Cut edges of each scale to point.

2 With craft knife, cut small hole in front of box. Hot-glue box lid closed. Paint entire surface of box Deep Lavender. Let dry. Repeat with another coat, if necessary, and let dry. Using True Yellow, paint stars and dots on box. Let dry.

3 Transfer roof pattern to cardboard and cut out. Overlap ends and hot-glue in place, leaving tiny hole at cone point for hanger. Using Burnt Umber, paint entire surface of cone roof. Let dry.

4 Hot-glue pinecone scales on cone roof, beginning with bottom edge. Layer and glue scales until roof is completely covered. For hanger, string 1 bead onto gold thread and position at center of thread. Fold thread in half to form loop and knot ends. Thread knotted end up through hole in roof. (Bead will keep hanger in hole.) String other beads from knotted end down to top of roof. Knot to secure beads. Center and hot-glue roof on box.

5 Randomly hot-glue sheet moss on roof and around birdhouse hole. Referring to photo at left, hot-glue 2 buttons together, one on top of other; using Black, paint 1 dot on top button for eye. Cut colored paper to make tail and beak; glue pieces in place on back of bird. Glue bird onto roof. Then paint 2 dots on 1 button for face and hot-glue to edge of hole (see photo on page 37).

Directions for red birdhouse

1 Follow Step 1 of directions for blue birdhouse. With craft knife, cut small hole in 1 side of juice can. Using True Red, paint entire surface of juice can. Let dry. Repeat with another coat if necessary. Let dry. Using Deep Lavender, paint dots around hole. Let dry. Using triangular sponge and Deep Green, stamp triangles along bottom edge of can for trees; outline triangles with Deep Green (see photo on page 37). Using True Yellow, paint stars and dots on can. Add stars to top of triangle trees. Let dry.

2 Complete steps 3 and 4 of directions for blue birdhouse. Randomly hot-glue sheet moss on roof and inside birdhouse hole. Referring to photo at left, hot-glue 2 buttons together, one on top of other; repeat to make another bird. Using Black, paint 1 dot on each bird head. Referring to Step 5 for blue birdhouse, finish each bird. Glue birds to birdhouse (see photo on page 37).

3 Tie ribbon in multilooped bow. Hot-glue ribbon to top of roof.

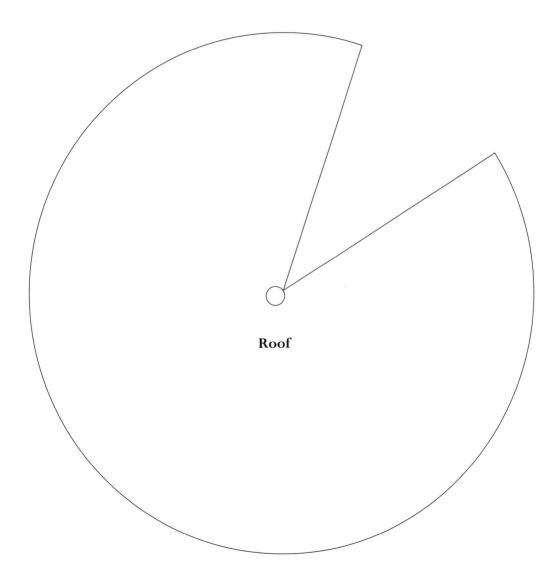

Roof

Angel Kitties

These ornaments are purr-fect for feline fanciers. All of the wooden shapes are purchased precut, so assembly couldn't be easier.

🐾 Materials 🐾

For each: 1 (3" x 6") piece posterboard
Aleene's Fusible Web™
1 (3" x 6") piece gold lamé fabric
Wooden shapes: 1 (1½"-diameter) half-round ball, 2 (¾"-wide and 1¼"-long) diamonds, 1 (1¾"-wide) heart
Aleene's Premium-Coat™ Acrylic Paints: True Red, Burnt Umber, Black
Aleene's Premium Designer Brushes™: shader, liner
Aleene's Designer Tacky Glue™
1 (7") length star garland
1 (8") length gold metallic thread
For gray kitty: Aleene's Premium-Coat™ Acrylic Paints: True Grey, Soft Grey
1 (1" x 12") torn green plaid strip fabric
½"-wide jeweled charm
For brown kitty: Aleene's Premium-Coat™ Acrylic Paint: Dusty Beige
5 gold stars
5 (4-mm) clear acrylic jewels
1 (12") length ⅞"-wide Christmas plaid ribbon

Directions

1 **For each,** transfer wings pattern to posterboard and cut out. Fuse web to wrong side of gold lamé. Center and fuse posterboard on fabric. Trim excess fabric from wings.

2 Paint half-round ball and diamonds True Grey or Dusty Beige; paint heart True Red. Let dry. Glue diamonds to back of half-round ball for kitty's ears. Let dry. **For gray kitty**, paint Soft Grey details using liner brush. **For brown kitty,** paint Burnt Umber details. **For each,** paint Burnt Umber nose and Black mouth. For eyes, dip handle of brush into Black and dot on kitty. Let dry.

3 Glue kitty head and heart on right side of wings. Curve star garland into 1½"-diameter circle and twist ends together. Bend twisted ends down at back of halo. Glue straight ends of halo to back of kitty head. For hanger, fold gold metallic thread in half and knot ends. Glue knot to back of kitty head. Let dry.

4 **For gray kitty,** tie fabric strip in bow. Glue bow to kitty at neck. Glue jeweled charm to bow. Let dry. **For brown kitty,** glue metallic stars and jewels to wings as desired. Let dry. Tie ribbon in bow. Glue bow to kitty at neck. Let dry.

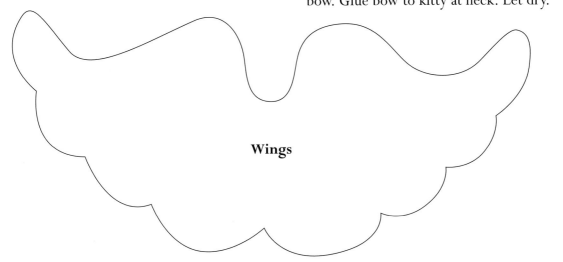

Wings

Bejeweled Christmas Accents

Turn your outdated or broken costume jewelry into glittering topiaries or ornaments. Showcase a favored charm or brooch, as Heidi did with the angel trio pin at the base of the topiary tree.

❧ Materials ❧

For each: Aleene's Designer Tacky Glue™
Florist's wire
Assorted pieces costume jewelry
Needlenose pliers (optional)
For topiary: Aleene's Premium-Coat™ Acrylic
  Paint: Gold
Sponge paintbrush
4½"-diameter clay flowerpot
Florist's foam
Craft Knife
1 (11") length ⅜"-diameter wooden dowel
1 (4") Styrofoam ball
Gold spray paint
Sheer ivory fabric
2 (36") lengths ¾"-wide sheer ribbon
For ornament: 3"-diameter satin-covered ball
  ornament
1 (36") length ½"-wide sheer ribbon
1 (10") length gold metallic thread

Note: Take jewelry pieces apart as needed, removing pin backs and earring findings with needlenose pliers.

Directions for topiary

1 Brush uneven coat of Gold on pot. Let dry. Using craft knife, cut florist's foam to fit inside pot. Glue foam inside pot. Center and push 1 end of dowel into foam in pot. Push free end of dowel halfway into Styrofoam ball. Spray-paint foam ball, dowel, and top of foam in pot gold. Let dry.

2 Cut 1 (15") square of sheer fabric. Wrap fabric square around foam ball to cover, gathering excess fabric around dowel at bottom of ball. Secure fabric around dowel with florist's wire. Trim fabric as desired. Arrange remaining fabric in decorative folds over foam in pot, gluing fabric in place as needed. Let dry.

3 Tie 1 ribbon length in bow at base of tree. Glue ribbon to pot as needed to secure. Tie remaining ribbon length in multilooped bow. Secure bow with florist's wire. Glue multilooped bow on top of first bow. Let dry.

4 Glue jewelry pieces to cover ball. Glue additional jewelry pieces to pot and base of topiary as desired. Let dry.

Directions for ornament

Glue jewelry pieces to cover ball. Let dry. Tie ribbon in multilooped bow. Secure bow with florist's wire, catching center of metallic thread in wire. Knot thread ends to form hanger. Glue bow to top of ornament. Let dry.

Search junk shops and yard sales to add to your stash of beads and baubles.

Angels by Nature

When you open your eyes to nature's beauty, you will see angels all around you. Here are three examples of a little bit of heaven on earth.

❧ Materials ❧

For each: Aleene's Ultimate Glue Gun™
Aleene's Hot Glue Sticks™: Floral
Gold metallic thread
For wheat angel: 1¼"-diameter wooden bead
    with hole
Aleene's Premium-Coat™ Acrylic Paint: Blush
Aleene's Premium Designer Brush™: shader
Fine-tip permanent black marker
Wooden skewer
Craft knife
Aleene's Botanical Preserved Flowers & Foliage™:
    Black Wisps Triticum, Natural Triticum, White
    Delphinium, Cedar
Florist's wire
1 (6") length ¼"-wide brown ribbon
For leaf angel: 1¼"-diameter wooden bead with
    hole
Aleene's Premium-Coat™ Acrylic Paint: Blush
Aleene's Premium Designer Brush™: shader
Fine-tip permanent black marker
Wooden skewer
Craft knife
Aleene's Botanical Preserved Flowers & Foliage™:
    Green Salal, Yellow Achillea Filipendulina
Gold spray paint
1 (12") length ⅛"-wide gold metallic ribbon
For pod angel: Aleene's Botanical Preserved
    Flowers & Foliage™: Natural Papaver, Natural
    Protea Flower
4 bay leaves
1 (12") length ½"-wide brown ribbon

Directions for wheat angel

1 Paint wooden bead with Blush. Let dry. Position bead so that hole is at top and bottom. Referring to photo and using permanent marker, draw face on side of head. Fill hole with hot glue. Working quickly, insert skewer into glue-filled hole. Let dry. Using craft knife, trim skewer to approximately 3½".

2 Referring to photo, gather triticum stalks together, with tips of stalks pointing down.

Insert skewer into center of stalk bunch. Wire stalks and skewer head piece together, using florist's wire. Trim stalks if needed. Use hot glue to help hold stalks together.

3 Referring to photo, hot-glue delphinium to top of head for hair and sprigs of cedar to back of angel for wings. Tie ribbon in bow and notch ends. Hot-glue bow to front of angel at neck.

4 For hanger, fold 12" length of gold thread in half to form loop and knot ends. Hot-glue knot to top back of angel.

Directions for leaf angel

1 Paint wooden bead with Blush. Let dry. Position bead so that hole is at top and bottom. Referring to photo and using permanent marker, draw face on side of head. Fill hole with hot glue. Working quickly, insert skewer into glue-filled hole. Let dry. Using craft knife, trim skewer to approximately 3½".

2 Spray-paint 2 medium-sized salal leaves gold. Let dry. Referring to photo and using large salal leaf for body and 4 small salal leaves for arms, hot-glue leaves together. Hot-glue gold salal leaf wings in place on back of body. Hot-glue skewer piece to back of body leaf piece.

3 Hot-glue achillea filipendulina to top of wooden bead for hair. Tie ribbon in bow. Hot-glue bow to front of angel at neck.

4 For hanger, fold 12" length of gold thread in half to form loop and knot ends. Hot-glue knot to top back of angel.

Directions for pod angel

1 Referring to photo, hot-glue papaver to base of protea and 4 bay leaves to back of protea for wings.

2 Tie ribbon in bow. Hot-glue bow to front of angel at neck.

3 For hanger, fold 12" length of gold thread in half to form loop and knot ends. Hot-glue knot to top back of angel.

Home Is Where the Heart Is

Page 68

Page 67

*E*legant frames, unique candle stands, and fragrant topiaries all add touches of joy to any home. Create one of these delightful gifts and then wrap it in love and tie it with heartstrings.

Page 59

Leafy Luxury

Mix and match print fabrics and stamped panels to cover purchased pillows for a sumptuous look. Create a grouping of oversize and smaller pillows for a truly luxurious gift.

Materials

For each: Aleene's Fusible Web™
Rubber bands
For large pillow with 4 fabric squares:
Fabrics: 4 (6½") squares ivy print, 2 (43") squares tan with gold flecks
1 (27") square European pillow
Aleene's Satin Sheen Twisted Ribbon™: beige, dark green
For large pillow with stamped-leaf square:
1 (5½" x 6½") piece Fun Foam
Woodburning tool
1 (5¾" x 7") piece foam-core board
Aleene's Designer Tacky Glue™
Fabrics: 1 (12") square tan with gold flecks, 2 (43") squares ivy print
Waxed paper
Aleene's Enhancers™ Textile Medium
Aleene's Premium-Coat™ Acrylic Paints: Deep Green, Deep Sage, Deep Khaki
Aleene's Premium Designer Brush™: shader
1 (27") square European pillow
4 (16") lengths 1½"-wide dark green wire-edged ribbon
For neck-roll pillow: Fabrics: 1 (5¼" x 8¼") piece off-white with gold speckles, 1 (37") square fern print
Waxed paper
1 silk fern leaf
Aleene's Enhancers™ Textile Medium
Aleene's Premium-Coat™ Acrylic Paints: Deep Green, Deep Sage, Deep Khaki
Aleene's Premium Designer Brush™: shader
1 (17") long neck-roll pillow
2 (18") lengths 1½"-wide sheer green ribbon

Directions for large pillow with 4 fabric squares

1 Wash and dry fabrics; do not use fabric softener in washer or dryer. Fuse web onto wrong side of each ivy print square. Referring to photo for positioning, fuse ivy squares to 1 gold-flecked square.

2 Lay remaining gold-flecked square wrong side up on work surface. Center pillow on square.

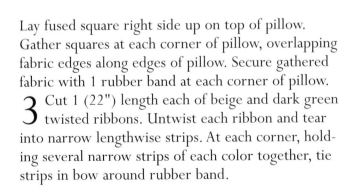

Lay fused square right side up on top of pillow. Gather squares at each corner of pillow, overlapping fabric edges along edges of pillow. Secure gathered fabric with 1 rubber band at each corner of pillow.

3 Cut 1 (22") length each of beige and dark green twisted ribbons. Untwist each ribbon and tear into narrow lengthwise strips. At each corner, holding several narrow strips of each color together, tie strips in bow around rubber band.

Directions for large pillow with stamped-leaf square

1 Transfer leaf pattern on page 50 to Fun Foam and cut out. Following manufacturer's directions, use woodburning tool to cut veins in foam

leaf as shown on pattern. Center and glue leaf on foam core. Let dry.

2 Wash and dry fabrics; do not use fabric softener in washer or dryer. Lay gold-flecked square right side up on work surface covered with waxed paper.

3 For each color of paint, mix equal parts textile medium and paint. Brush paints on stamp as desired. Position stamp on fabric in desired position and press firmly, making sure all areas of stamp come in contact with fabric. Lift stamp off fabric. Move stamp to another position and press onto fabric without reapplying paint (see photo). Repeat to stamp 4 more leaves on fabric. Let dry.

4 Fuse web onto wrong side of stamped fabric. Center and fuse stamped fabric on right side of 1 ivy print square.

5 Refer to Step 2 of directions for large pillow with 4 fabric squares to cover pillow with fabric pieces. Tie 1 ribbon length in bow around each rubber band.

Directions for neck-roll pillow

1 Wash and dry fabrics; do not use fabric softener in washer or dryer. Lay gold-speckled fabric right side up on waxed paper-covered work surface.

2 Referring to Step 3 of directions for large pillow with stamped-leaf square, brush thin coat of desired paints on 1 side of silk leaf. Press painted side of leaf onto gold-speckled fabric in desired position. Carefully remove leaf without smudging paint. Repeat to paint 2 more leaves on fabric (see photo). Let dry.

3 Fuse web onto wrong side of painted fabric. Center painted fabric on width of fern print fabric, with 1 long edge of painted fabric parallel to and 11½" from 1 end of fern print fabric. Fuse painted fabric to right side of fern print fabric.

4 Beginning at other end of fern print fabric, roll neck-roll pillow inside fabric. Gather fabric at each end of pillow and secure with rubber bands. Tie 1 ribbon length in bow around each rubber band.

Leaf

Wire Art Frames

Who says picture frames have to be wooden rectangles? These playful pieces are as much artwork as they are functional frames.

☙ Materials ☙
(for each frame)
Drill with ¹⁄₁₆" bit
Wooden finial or plaque
Needlenose pliers
16- to 18-gauge wire
Wire cutters
Gold spray paint
Aleene's Ultimate Glue Gun™
Aleene's Glue Sticks™: All-Purpose
Variety beads
Eye pins
Jump rings
Variety multicolored embroidery floss
Ribbon

Directions

1. For base, drill hole in top of wooden finial or drill holes in wooden plaque, spacing holes as desired.

2. For each wire stand, refer to photo and use needlenose pliers to bend wire into spirals, leaving straight stem at 1 end of wire. Trim wire with wire cutters.

3. Spray-paint wooden base and wire stands gold. Let dry. For each wire stand, apply hot glue to straight end of wire. Working quickly, insert wire stand into 1 hole in wooden base.

4. Attach beads and eye pins to wire stands, using jump rings. Tie floss and ribbon to wire stands as desired. Slip photos between loops in spirals.

Floral Door Mat

Greet a new neighbor with this nifty mat. If desired, replace
"Welcome" with the family's name.

Materials

Aleene's Opake Shrink-It™ Plastic
Craft knife
Masking tape
Natural-fiber outdoor mat
Aleene's Premium-Coat™ Acrylic Paints: Light Fuchsia, Medium Fuchsia, True Fuchsia, Deep Fuchsia, Medium Violet, True Violet, Deep Violet, Deep Sage, Dusty Sage, Deep Green, Light Blue, True Blue
Paintbrushes: 1 round stencil, ½" flat shader
4" alphabet stencils

Directions

1 For each pattern, cut 1 piece of Shrink-It, 1" larger all around than pattern. Center and transfer pattern on corresponding piece of Shrink-It. Cut out 1 flower and 1 leaf. Set cutouts aside for another use.

2 Referring to photo for positioning and color, tape 1 stencil where desired on wrong side of mat. Apply paint inside stencil area, using stencil brush. Let dry. Repeat to stencil letters, flowers, and leaves on mat. For shaded effect, stencil part of flower or leaf with light shade and then stencil remaining part of design with darker shade. To paint dots, dip 1 edge of stencil brush into Light Blue and then dip other edge into True Blue. Press onto mat in desired position. To paint details and to outline flowers and leaves, use ½" flat shader brush. Let dry.

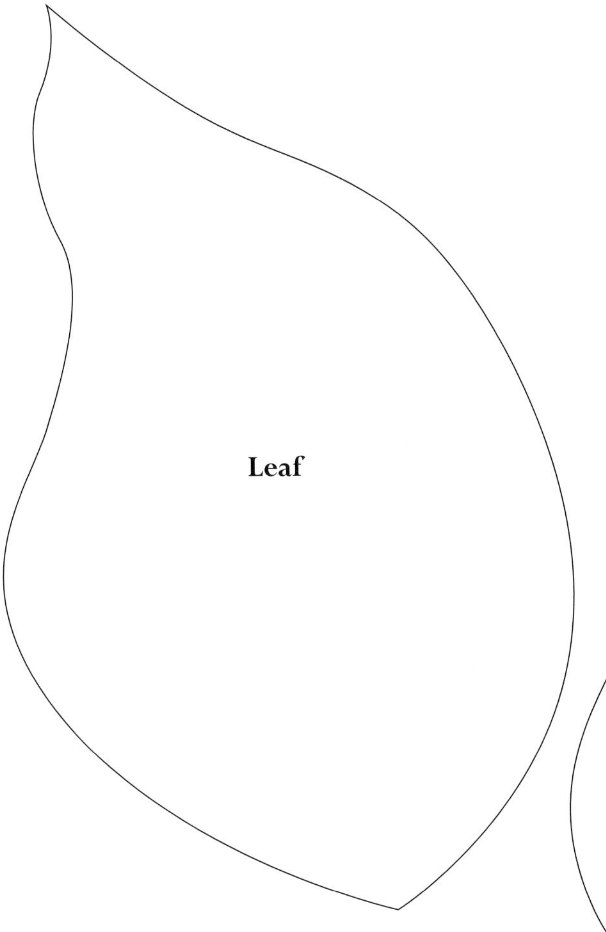

Leaf

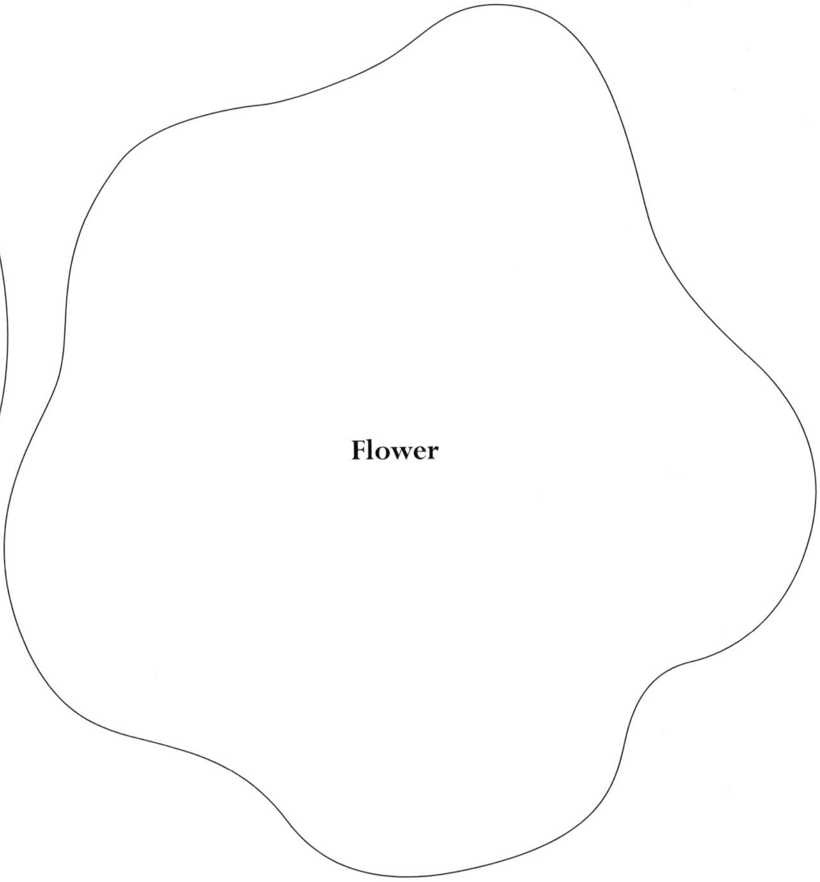

Flower

Natural Home Delights

*These earthy accents work equally well with an elegant or rustic decor.
The natural frames are a great showcase
for outdoor adventure photos.*

*Naturally, this frame needs a
finishing touch. Heidi clustered a few
sprigs of evergreen, some dried flowers, and several miniature pinecones
in a couple of corners.*

Create a matching needle-covered lampshade for a dramatic grouping on a side table.

❧ Materials ❧

For each: Hot-glue gun and glue sticks
For pine-needle frame: Aleene's Reverse
   Collage™ Glue
Paintbrush
Black mat with oval cutout to fit frame
Dried pine needles
Wooden frame
Assorted dried naturals
For wheat-sheaves frame: Gold spray paint
Mat with oval cutout to fit frame
Wheat sheaves
Raffia
Wooden frame
For pine-needle lampshade: Gold spray paint
Lampshade
Dried pine needles

Directions for pine-needle frame

Working over small area at a time, brush coat of Reverse Collage Glue onto right side of mat. Press pine needles into glue at angle (see photo on page 54). Brush coat of glue on top of pine needles. Repeat until mat is covered. Let dry. Hot-glue mat to inside of frame back. Hot-glue other naturals to mat as desired.

Directions for wheat-sheaves frame

Spray-paint mat gold. Let dry. Snap off enough heads from wheat sheaves to cover mat. Hot-glue wheat heads to edge of oval cutout (see photo below). Then glue wheat heads in vertical lines to cover mat. Fill any spaces with wheat stems.

Tie raffia in bow. Hot-glue raffia to center top of mat. Hot-glue mat to inside of frame back.

Directions for pine-needle lampshade

Spray-paint shade gold. Let dry. Hot-glue pine needles vertically onto shade, beginning at top edge and gluing tips of needles only. Layer pine needles on top of each other until shade is covered, with last layer of pine needles overhanging lower edge of shade freely. Trim needles if necessary.

*Depending
on where you live, wheat
sheaves may be more readily available
than pine for making frames. The look
is equally effective.*

Busy Bee Place Setting

Bring the feeling of a bright summer garden to a friend's kitchen table.
She will buzz about the bee-utiful place settings you made for her.

❧ Materials ❧

For each: Aleene's Fusible Web™
Dimensional fabric paints: black, white
For each place mat: Fabrics: scraps for appliqués,
    1 (5") square and 1 (11½" x 15¾") piece denim
Aleene's OK to Wash-It™ Glue
Sponge paintbrush
Aleene's Paper Napkin Appliqué™ Glue
1 (12" x 16") piece white Fun Foam
For each napkin: Fabrics: scraps for appliqués,
    1 (14½") square yellow plaid
For each napkin ring: Fabrics: 1 (16") and 1 (21")
    length 1"-wide strips yellow, yellow and white
    scraps
1 (1"-wide) piece cardboard paper towel tube
Aleene's Ultimate Glue Gun™
Aleene's Glue Sticks™: All-Purpose
Aleene's Premium-Coat™ Acrylic Paints: Black, White
Sponge paintbrush
Wooden cutouts: 1 (¾")-diameter circle, 1 (2")-
    long oval, 2 (1"-wide) hearts
Needlenose pliers
1 (2") length 18-gauge wire

Directions for place mat

1 Press fusible web onto wrong side of fabric scraps. Referring to photo for colors, transfer patterns below and on page 58 to paper side of fabric scraps. Cut out shapes.

2 Slightly fray edges of both denim pieces. For pocket, fuse shapes in place on 5" denim square (see photo). Paint eyes and antennas with dimensional paints. Let dry. Apply thin line of OK to Wash-It Glue along bottom and side edges of pocket. Position pocket in lower right-hand corner of 11½" x 15¾" denim piece. Referring to photo, fuse remaining shapes in place on left-hand side of place mat. Paint eyes and antennas with dimensional paints. Let dry.

3 Using sponge brush, apply coat of Napkin Appliqué Glue to 1 side of Fun Foam. Center place mat faceup on foam. Smooth out wrinkles. Apply coat of Napkin Appliqué Glue to top of place mat. Let dry.

Directions for napkin

1 Press fusible web onto wrong side of fabric scraps. Referring to photo for colors, transfer patterns on page 58 to paper side of fabric scraps. Cut out shapes.

2 Slightly fray all edges of 14½" yellow square. Fuse shapes in place on upper right-hand corner of yellow square (see photo). Paint eyes and antennas with dimensional paints. Let dry.

Flower

Flower Center

Tulip

Leaf

Picket Fence Post

Picket Fence Cross Post

Heidi fused yellow fabric stripes on the bee's body and white fabric hearts on the bee's wings. However, if you prefer, use acrylic paint for the stripes and the wings.

Directions for napkin ring

1 Slightly fray edges of yellow fabric strips. Wrap 21" yellow strip around cardboard tube section and hot-glue in place. Tie remaining fabric strip in bow. Hot-glue bow on wrapped ring to cover over-lapped ends.

2 Paint wooden circle and oval Black and hearts White. Let dry.

3 Press fusible web onto wrong side of fabric scraps. Referring to photo for colors, transfer stripes and wings patterns to paper side of fabric scraps. Cut out shapes. Referring to photo, fuse stripes in place on oval. Fuse wings in place on hearts.

4 Using needlenose pliers, curl each end of wire length. Bend wire length in half. Hot-glue wings and head in place on oval. For antennas, hot-glue wire at top back of head. Paint bee's eyes with dimensional paint. Let dry. Hot-glue bee to bow.

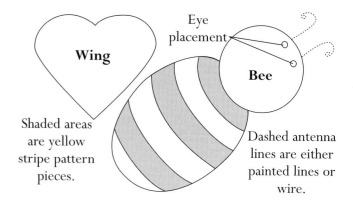

Wing

Shaded areas are yellow stripe pattern pieces.

Eye placement

Bee

Dashed antenna lines are either painted lines or wire.

Spice Topiaries

These topiaries add spice to any home decor. Heidi used coriander seeds, mustard seeds, bay leaves, and black peppercorns (left to right in the photo), but you can use whichever spices or seeds you have on hand.

❧ Materials ❧

For each: Aleene's Designer Tacky Glue™
Florist's foam block to fit inside clay pot
Sheet moss

For bay-leaves topiary: Toothpick
1 (1") wooden star with small hole in bottom
Gold spray paint
1 (8"-tall) Styrofoam cone
Craft knife
1 (10") length ¼"-diameter wooden dowel
Clay pot (4¼" tall and 4¼" in diameter at top)
Bay leaves
1 (36") length 1½"-wide gold ribbon

For mustard-seed topiary: 1 (1½"-diameter)
  Styrofoam ball
Ground cinnamon
1 (2½") length bamboo skewer
Aleene's Premium-Coat™ Acrylic Paint: Deep Sage
Aleene's Premium Designer Brush™: shader
Clay pot (1⅝" tall and 1⅝" in diameter at top)
Mustard seeds
⅛"-wide gold ribbon: 1 (5¾") length, 1 (5") length

For peppercorn topiary: 1 (2¼"-diameter)
  Styrofoam ball
Ground cinnamon
1 (4½") length ¼"-diameter wooden dowel
Aleene's Premium-Coat™ Acrylic Paint: Deep Sage
Aleene's Premium Designer Brush™: shader
Clay pot (2½" tall and 2½" in diameter at top)
Black peppercorns
Raffia

For coriander topiary: 1 (7"-tall) Styrofoam
  cone
Craft knife
1 (8") length ¼"-diameter wooden dowel
Gold spray paint
Clay pot (3½" tall and 3½" in diameter at top)
Coriander
1 (11") length ⅝"-wide green ribbon
Raffia
Straight pin

Directions for bay-leaves topiary

1 Dip 1 end of toothpick into glue and push into hole in star. Let dry. Spray star and toothpick gold. Let dry. Cut off tip of cone. Spray cone and dowel gold. Let dry.

2 Glue foam block inside pot. Dip 1 end of dowel into glue and push into bottom of cone. Dip free end of dowel into glue and push into foam in pot. Let dry. Glue moss to cover foam in pot. Let dry.

3 With tip of each leaf pointing down and stem end of each leaf about ¾" above bottom of cone, glue leaves around bottom of cone, overlapping leaves slightly. In same manner, glue another row of leaves around cone, about 1¾" above first row; continue adding rows of leaves to completely cover cone (see photo above). For final row of leaves, fold and glue stem end of leaves over top of cone. Let dry. Dip free end of star-topped toothpick into glue and push into top of cone. Let dry.

4 Wrap and glue ribbon around pot. Tie ribbon ends in bow at front of pot. Let dry.

Directions for mustard-seed topiary

1 Spread even coat of glue on ball. Roll glue-covered ball in ground cinnamon to coat. Let dry. Paint skewer Deep Sage. Let dry. Repeat Step 2 of directions for bay-leaves topiary, using skewer instead of dowel.

2 Spread fairly thick coat of glue over surface of cinnamon-covered ball. Press mustard seeds into glue to completely cover ball. Let dry.

3 Wrap and glue 5¾" ribbon around top of pot. Tie remaining ribbon in bow and glue bow to pot at front of topiary. Let dry.

Directions for coriander topiary

1 Cut off tip of cone to flatten. Spray cone and dowel gold. Let dry. Repeat Step 2 of directions for bay-leaves topiary.

2 Spread fairly thick coat of glue over surface of cone. Press coriander into glue to completely cover cone. Let dry.

3 Glue ribbon around rim of pot. Tie several lengths of raffia in bow. Pin bow to base of cone near dowel.

Directions for peppercorn topiary

1 Spread even coat of glue on ball. Roll glue-covered ball in ground cinnamon to coat. Let dry. Paint dowel Deep Sage. Let dry. Repeat Step 2 of directions for bay-leaves topiary.

2 Spread fairly thick coat of glue over surface of cinnamon-covered ball. Press peppercorns into glue to completely cover ball. Let dry.

3 Cut several 10" lengths of raffia. Holding lengths together, tie raffia in bow. Glue bow to moss-covered foam at base of dowel. Let dry.

Because mustard seeds are so small, they are a good choice for miniature topiaries.

Tabletop Tiles

A thoughtful housewarming gift, these clay tile trivets and coasters will protect the recipient's counter or table. Use the pattern provided to make your stamp or, if you prefer, cut a different shape freehand. Either way, the application is the same.

❧ Materials ☙

For each: Aleene's Premium-Coat™ Acrylic Paints:
   Dusty Blush, Deep Blush, Dusty Peach, Ivory
Sponge paintbrush
Waxed paper
Natural sea sponge
Fun Foam scrap
Foam-core board scrap
Aleene's Designer Tacky Glue™
Aleene's Premium Designer Brush™: shader
Clear spray sealer
For coaster: 1 (4¼") square clay tile
4 self-adhesive rubber bumper pads (optional)
For trivet: 1 (11⅝") square clay tile
4 (¾") wooden beads

Directions for coaster

1 Wash and dry right side of tile. Paint right side with 1 or 2 coats of Dusty Blush, letting dry between coats. Pour separate puddles of Deep Blush and Dusty Peach onto waxed paper. Dip dampened natural sponge into both puddles of paint for mottled effect. Sponge-paint right side of tile. Let dry.

2 To make stamp, transfer pattern on page 64 to Fun Foam and cut out. Cut 1 piece of foam-core board, ½" larger all around than pattern. Center and glue foam piece onto foam core. Let dry. Brush coat of Ivory onto stamp.

3 Place stamp on tile and press firmly, making sure all areas of stamp come in contact with tile. Carefully lift stamp off tile. Let dry. If desired, adhere 1 rubber bumper at each corner on wrong side of tile.

4 Spray right side of tile with 1 or 2 coats of sealer, letting dry between coats.

Directions for trivet

1 Follow steps 1 and 2 of directions for coaster. Referring to photo for positioning, place stamp on tile and press firmly, making sure all areas of stamp come in contact with tile. Carefully lift stamp off tile. Let dry. Repeat to complete design, applying fresh coat of paint before each stamping.

2 Glue 1 wooden bead on wrong side of tile at each corner.

3 To complete trivet, follow Step 4 of directions for coaster.

Stamp
Cut out shaded areas of design.

Birdhouse Decorative Pillows

These throw pillows are charming accents for a settee on a sun porch or a couch in a den. Use flannel and muted felts for a warm, folksy feel or cotton chintz and bright felts for a whimsical touch.

❧ Materials ❧
(for 1 pillow)

Fabrics: 2 (11" x 18½") pieces for pillow, 1 (7½")
   square for roof

Aleene's Fusible Web™

Felt: 1 (8" x 11") piece for birdhouse, 1 (8½") square
   for roof, 1 (2" x 6") piece for holes, 1 (2" x 9") piece
   for leaves, 1 (4" x 5") piece for bird, scrap for beak

Embroidery floss in desired color and embroidery
   needle

1 black half-round bead eye or ¼" wooden bead

Aleene's Tacky Glue™

Stuffing

Thread to match pillow

Directions

1 Measure and mark midpoint along 1 short edge of
1 (11" x 18½") pillow piece. Measure and mark
11" from opposite short edge along each side. Referring
to Diagram, draw diagonal lines extending from midpoint to each marked point along sides. Cut along
marked lines. Repeat with remaining 11" x 18½" piece.

2 Press fusible web onto wrong side of 7½" fabric
square and each felt piece. Cut fabric square and
8½" felt square in half diagonally to form triangular
roof pieces. (You will use only 1 felt triangle piece and
1 fabric triangle piece; set aside remaining triangle
pieces for another project.) Cut 2 or 3 (1⅝"-diameter)
circles from 2" x 6" felt piece. Transfer leaf pattern 2 or
3 times to 2" x 9" felt piece, bird pattern to 4" x 5" felt
piece, and beak pattern to felt scrap. Cut out shapes.

3 Remove paper backing from triangular fabric piece
only. Center fabric triangle on felt triangle and fuse
in place. Remove paper backing from all felt pieces.
Referring to photo, fuse birdhouse, roof, holes, leaves,
bird, and beak onto right side of 1 fabric birdhouse.

4 Referring to photo, use embroidery needle and
floss to straightstitch or buttonhole-stitch around
shapes. Use straight stitches to make veins along center
of leaves. Glue eye in place. Let dry.

5 With right sides facing and edges aligned, stitch
birdhouses together, using ¼" seam allowance and
leaving 5" along bottom edge unstitched. Stuff pillow
through opening. Slipstitch opening closed.

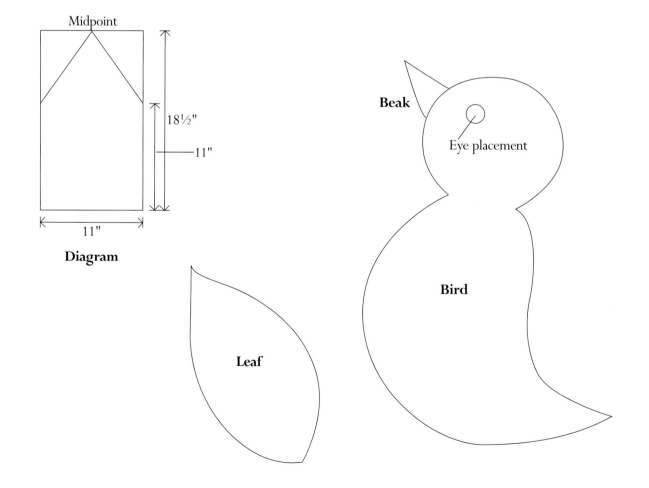

Midpoint

18½"

11"

11"

Diagram

Leaf

Beak

Eye placement

Bird

Ivy Accents

Trailing ivy vines add a touch of elegant simplicity to a plain frame or vase. The look is both classic and versatile.

～ Materials ～

For each: Paintbrush
Silk ivy leaves
Aleene's Reverse Collage™ Glue
Aleene's 3-D Foiling™ Glue
Aleene's Gold Crafting Foil™
For frame: Clear acrylic frame
For vase: Plain glass vase

Directions

1 **For frame,** use paintbrush to coat backs of silk leaves with Reverse Collage Glue. Referring to photo, arrange leaves on frame as desired. Let dry.

2 Outline leaves and draw veins and vines with 3-D Foiling Glue. Let dry. (Glue will be sticky when dry. Glue must be thoroughly dry when foil is applied.) To apply gold foil, lay foil dull side down on top of glue lines. Using finger, press foil onto glue, completely covering glue with foil. Peel away foil paper.

3 **For vase,** apply leaves to side of vase (see Step 1). Let dry. Refer to Step 2 to outline leaves and to add veins and vines.

Put Them on a Pedestal

You may have seen such pedestals offered for sale in catalogs. With these directions, you can make a set in an afternoon, saving time and money.

Materials
(for 3 pedestals)
Wood: 1 (6" x 6" x 5") piece, 1 (6" x 6" x 3")
    piece, 1 (4" x 4" x 6¼") piece
Fine-grade sandpaper
Tack cloth
Aleene's True Snow™
Palette knife
Small plastic paint comb (optional)
Assorted silk or real leaves
Aleene's Enhancers™ Clear Gel Medium
Aleene's Premium-Coat™ Acrylic Paints: Yellow
    Ochre, Burnt Umber, Deep Sage
Aleene's Premium Designer Brush™: shader
Clear spray sealer

Directions

1 **For each,** sand wooden piece smooth. Wipe piece with tack cloth to remove any dust. Apply True Snow to sides of pedestal for textured surface, using palette knife. If desired, rake comb across wet surface to add more texture. Apply thin coat of True Snow to back of each leaf. Press leaves into wet surface of pedestal to adhere to wood. Let dry.

2 Mix 2 parts Clear Gel Medium with 1 part desired color of paint. Brush paint mixture over entire surface of pedestal for desired effect. Let dry.

3 Spray pedestal with 1 or 2 coats of sealer, letting dry between coats.

Dream Pillow

Bathe a bedroom in moonlight and the relaxing aroma of potpourri with this celestial herb-filled pillow. Sprinkle sweet herbs into the pillow's lining to give it a heavenly scent that will conjure sweet dreams.

Materials

Sponge paintbrush
Fabrics: 1 (12") square muslin; 2 (8") and 2 (16")
    squares ivory; 4 (1" x 18") torn fabric strips
Aleene's Thin-Bodied Tacky Glue™
Aleene's Premium-Coat™ Acrylic Paints: True
    Lavender, Medium Yellow, True Orange
Aleene's Premium Designer Brush™: shader
Gold glitter dimensional fabric paint
Thread: gold metallic, ivory
1 (12") pillow form
Dried herbs (See sample recipe below.)
Hand-sewing needle

Directions

1 Using sponge brush, paint 1 side of muslin square with Thin-Bodied Tacky Glue. Let dry. (Glue will act as resist to paint.) Thoroughly wash sponge brush.

2 Referring to photo, use sponge brush and True Lavender to paint sky on prepared muslin square. (Use light strokes and small amount of paint to achieve watercolor effect.) Let dry. Use sponge brush and Medium Yellow to paint moon. Let dry. Use shader brush, True Lavender, and True Orange to paint facial details on moon. Let dry. Use gold glitter dimensional paint to paint stars and "Dream." Let dry.

3 Center muslin square right side up on right side of 1 (16") fabric square. Using metallic thread and sewing machine, zigzag along edges of muslin square.

4 With right sides facing and raw edges aligned, use ivory thread to machine-stitch 16" fabric squares together, using ½" seam allowance and leaving 1 side open. Turn right side out. Repeat to stitch 8" fabric squares together. Turn.

5 Insert pillow form into pillow casing. Fill pouch with dried herbs. Using hand-sewing needle and ivory thread, slipstitch opening in herb pouch closed. Insert herb pouch into pillow. Slipstitch opening in pillow closed.

6 Tie each fabric strip in bow. Referring to photo and using hand-sewing needle and ivory thread, tack 1 bow to each corner of painted muslin square.

Herb Potpourri

If you have a favorite herb, such as lavender, you may choose to fill the pillow with only that herb. However, a potpourri of herbs can create a unique and soothing aroma. This recipe is one of Heidi's favorites. All of the herbs it requires can be purchased from Heidi's sister Candace Liccione at The Herbal Sanctuary, 426 Fruit Farm Road, Royersford, PA 19468.

½ cup rosebuds and rose petals
1 cup chamomile firs
1 cup mugwort leaves
½ cup lavender firs
1 cup hops flowers
¼ cup rosemary leaves

Guardian Angels

Protect your loved ones with the soft, reassuring glow from a night-light. Simply decorate a purchased light with a faux stained-glass cherub dressed in colors to match the hallway or bathroom. An angel to guard a nursery or child's bedroom makes an especially thoughtful gift.

❧ Materials ❧
(for both angels)
Aleene's Crafting Plastic™
Aleene's 3-D Foiling Glue™
Aleene's Gold Crafting Foil™
Aleene's Tissue Paper™: pink, red, purple, light
   blue, white, yellow, gold
Aleene's Reverse Collage Glue™
Aleene's Premium Designer Brush™: shader
Fine-tip permanent black marker
2 night-lights
Aleene's Designer Tacky Glue™

Directions
Note: Adjust size of cutout on cloud piece as needed
to fit your night-light switch.

1 Transfer patterns to plastic and cut 1 girl, 1 boy,
2 clouds, and 6 stars. Referring to photos and
patterns, apply lines of 3-D Foiling Glue to right
side of each plastic design to outline shape and to
add details. Let dry. (Glue will be sticky when dry.
Glue must be thoroughly dry before foil is applied.)
To apply gold foil, lay foil dull side down on top of
glue lines. Using your finger, press foil onto glue,
completely covering glue with foil. Peel away foil
paper.

2 **For girl,** tear narrow strips of pink and red tissue paper to cover dress and feet. **For boy,**
transfer patterns to tissue paper; cut 1 shirt from purple, 1 pants from light blue, and 2 feet from white.

Star

Boy

Girl

Cloud

Cut out.

Depending on the color of tissue paper you choose for your angel, this could be a holiday decoration or a year-round accent.

For each, transfer patterns to tissue paper; cut 1 face and 2 hands from white, hair from yellow, and wings from gold. Transfer patterns to tissue paper and cut 2 clouds from white and 6 stars from yellow.

3 **For girl,** brush coat of Reverse Collage Glue on wrong side of dress. Press pink and red paper strips into glue, layering paper strips to get desired effect. In same manner, glue paper pieces on wrong side of girl to cover feet. Crumple each remaining paper piece and then flatten it, leaving some wrinkles. Glue remaining paper pieces in place on wrong side of matching plastic pieces, using Reverse Collage Glue. Let dry. **For boy,** crumple each paper piece and then flatten it, leaving some wrinkles. Glue paper pieces in place on wrong side of matching plastic pieces, using Reverse Collage Glue. Let dry

4 **For each,** referring to patterns, draw facial features, using marker. Referring to photos, glue 1 cloud, 1 angel, and 3 stars to each night-light, using Designer Tacky Glue. Let dry.

Birdhouse Welcome Mat

The sights of an early spring inspired this canvas floor mat.
All the designs are sponge-painted, so it's a very easy project.

❧ Materials ℘

Aleene's Premium Designer Brushes™: shader, liner
Aleene's Premium-Coat™ Acrylic Paints: Light Blue, Ivory, True Violet, Deep Mauve, Deep Lavender, Burnt Umber, Deep Beige, Deep Blush, Black, True Apricot, Deep Sage, True Yellow
Purchased half-round canvas rug (about 37" long and 18⅜" wide)
Pop-up craft sponges
Waxed paper
Precut sponge letters: E, H, M, O, S, T, W
Clear polyurethane spray

Instructions

1 Dip shader brush into Light Blue and Ivory and paint right side of canvas rug to look like sky. Let dry.

2 Transfer patterns to pop-up sponges and cut 1 large roof, 1 small roof, 1 flower, 1 leaf, and 1 heart; also cut 1 (¾" x 5½") piece for fence picket, 1 (2½" x 2¾") piece for birdhouse A, 1 (2" x 4½") piece for birdhouse B, 1 (1½" x 3¼") piece for birdhouse C, 1 (¾"-diameter) circle, and 1 (½"-diameter) circle. Trim 1 end of ¾" x 5½" fence picket piece to form point. Dip each sponge into water to expand and wring out excess water.

3 Pour separate puddles for each color of paint onto waxed paper. Dip each dampened sponge into desired color of paint. (Rinse each sponge thoroughly before dipping into different color.) Referring to photo for placement and leaving about ½" between each, sponge-paint 17 fence pickets along curved edge of canvas with Ivory. Use end of fence picket sponge to sponge-paint crossbars of fence. Let dry.

4 Referring to photo for placement, sponge-paint birdhouse A with True Violet, birdhouse B with Deep Mauve, and birdhouse C with Deep Lavender. Let dry. Sponge-paint large roof on birdhouse A with Burnt Umber, large roof on birdhouse B with Deep Beige, and small roof on birdhouse C with Deep Blush. Sponge-paint post on each birdhouse with Burnt Umber, using 1 edge of large roof sponge piece. Let dry.

5 Sponge-paint 1 (¾") Black circle and 1 Deep Mauve heart on birdhouse A, 2 (¾") Black circles on birdhouse B, and 3 (½") Black circles on birdhouse C. Let dry.

6 Referring to photo, sponge-paint True Apricot flowers and Deep Sage leaves on canvas as desired. Sponge-paint letters Deep Mauve. Let dry. Sponge-paint 1 (½") Burnt Umber circle on each flower for center. Let dry. Sponge-paint 1 (¾") True Yellow circle on top of each Burnt Umber circle. Let dry.

7 Referring to photo, add details to painted designs, using paint colors as desired and liner brush. Let dry. To paint dot flowers, dip handle of liner brush into Ivory and press onto canvas. In same manner, dip brush into True Apricot to add center to each dot flower. Let dry.

8 Spray rug with 1 or 2 coats of sealer, letting dry between coats.

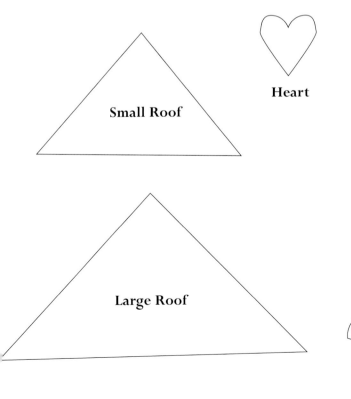

Small Roof

Heart

Large Roof

Flower

Leaf

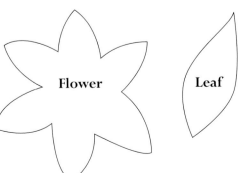

For the Birds

While planning your garden, consider planting flowers, shrubs, and vines that will bring birds to your yard; such foliage includes honeysuckle, rose, and rosemary. If hummingbirds are your favorite, try planting geraniums, gladiolus, hollyhocks, or impatiens.

Personal Style

Page 98

Page 90

Because a friend is a gift to treasure forever, brighten her day as you brighten her wardrobe with one of the treasures found in this chapter. A frilly white vest, a ribbon rose-adorned sweater and purse, or a feminine shirt will make her feel pretty and special.

Page 78

Collar Art

A profusion of ribbon flowers takes a plain white blouse to a new dimension, and buttons add interesting texture to a denim shirt. If you don't have lots of flowers or buttons, consider gluing just one decorative row along the collar edge instead of covering the collar as Heidi did.

❧ Materials ❧

Shirt with collar
Aleene's Jewel-It Glue™
Assorted ribbon flowers or buttons
⅛"-wide ecru satin ribbon (optional)

Directions

1 **For each,** wash and dry shirt. Do not use fabric softener in washer or dryer.

2 **For flowers shirt,** apply glue to bottom of 1 flower and press onto shirt collar where desired. Repeat to cover shirt collar. Let dry. If desired, cut and glue lengths of ecru ribbon to add detail to shirt front (see photo). Glue ribbon flowers on top of ribbon, spacing flowers about 1" apart. Let dry.

3 **For buttons shirt,** squeeze puddle of glue on shirt collar in desired position. Press 1 button into glue so that glue comes up around sides of button and through holes. Repeat to cover shirt collar. Let dry. If desired, glue buttons to decorate top edge of shirt pocket (see photo). Let dry.

4 **For each,** do not wash shirt for at least 1 week. Turn shirt wrong side out, wash by hand, and hang to dry.

Photo Charms

Any grandmother would love to accessorize an outfit with one of these charms—especially if the photos they feature are of her grandchildren. The charms are easy and inexpensive to create from Shrink-It.

❧ Materials ❧

For each: Aleene's Opake Shrink-It™ Plastic
Fine-grade sandpaper
Fine-tip permanent black marker
Aleene's Baking Board or nonstick cookie sheet,
    sprinkled with baby powder
Aleene's Designer Tacky Glue™
Miniature photos
For pin: Colored pencils
³⁄₁₆" hole punch
Silver spray paint
Dimensional paints
Aleene's Craft Tools™: needlenose pliers
Jump rings
Charm pin
For necklace: ³⁄₁₆" hole punch
Gold spray paint
Aleene's Craft Tools™: needlenose pliers
Jump rings
Necklace chain
For earrings: Gold spray paint
2 earring backs

Directions

1 For each, sand 1 side of each piece of
Shrink-It so that markings will adhere. Be
sure to thoroughly sand both vertically and
horizontally. Using black marker, trace desired
patterns onto sanded side of Shrink-It. (**For earrings,** do *not* transfer loop on top of charm
shape.) Referring to photo and using black
marker, draw designs on heart charms if desired.
(Marker ink may run on sanded surface; runs
will shrink and disappear during baking.)

2 **For pin,** use colored pencils to color each heart design. (Remember that colors will be more intense after shrinking.) **For each,** cut out charm shapes. (**For necklace and pin,** punch holes where designated in charm shapes.) Preheat toaster oven or conventional oven to 275° to 300°. Place each design on room-temperature baking board and bake in oven. Edges should begin to curl within 25 seconds; if not, increase temperature slightly. If edges begin to curl as soon as designs are put in oven, reduce temperature. After about 1 minute, designs will lie flat. Remove each design from oven. Let cool.

3 **For necklace,** spray-paint charm gold. Let dry. Use needlenose pliers to attach charm to necklace chain with jump rings. Glue photo to back of charm.

4 **For earrings,** spray-paint charms gold. Let dry. Glue photo to back of each charm. Let dry. Glue earring back to back of photo. Let dry.

5 **For pin,** spray-paint rectangular charm silver. Let dry. Embellish charms with dimensional paints as desired; glue photo to back of rectangular charm. Let dry. Use needlenose pliers to attach charms to charm pin with jump rings.

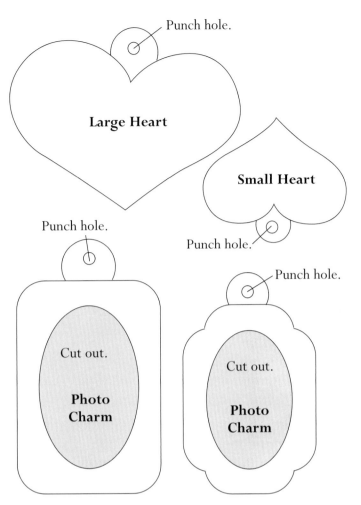

Punch hole.

Large Heart

Small Heart

Punch hole.

Punch hole.

Punch hole.

Cut out.

Photo Charm

Cut out.

Photo Charm

Hearts-Allover Jewelry Set

These lightweight earrings and necklace look spectacular against a black sweater or dress. The matching jewelry box completes the gift set.

❧ Materials ❧

For each: Aleene's Opake Shrink-It™ Plastic
Aleene's Baking Board or nonstick cookie sheet, sprinkled with baby powder
Embossing fluid
Paintbrushes
Embossing powder: gold, silver glitter, green, red, black
Hair dryer or embossing heat tool
Swirl rubber stamp
Embossing ink pad
For necklace ⅛" hole punch
Assorted ¼"-round beads
Jump rings: 1 (½"-diameter), 1 (¼"-diameter)
Aleene's Craft Tools™: needlenose pliers
1¼ yards ¼"-wide ribbon
For earrings: Embossing pen
⅛" hole punch
Jump rings: 2 (¼"-diameter), 2 (½"-diameter)
Assorted ¼"-round beads
Aleene's Craft Tools™: needlenose pliers
1 pair fishhook earrings
For jewelry box: Aleene's Premium-Coat™ Acrylic Paint: Black
6"-square papier-mâché box
Embossing pen
5 (1½"-diameter) wooden craft balls
Star rubber stamp
Aleene's Ultimate Glue Gun™
Aleene's All-Purpose Glue Sticks™

Directions for necklace

1 Transfer 1 medium heart and 1 large heart patterns (on page 84) to Shrink-It. Cut out. Punch 1 hole at top center of medium heart and 1 hole each at top center and bottom center of large heart.

2 Preheat toaster oven or conventional oven to 275° to 300°. Place each design on room-temperature baking board and bake in oven. Edges should begin to curl within 25 seconds; if not, increase temperature slightly. If edges begin to curl as soon as designs are put in oven, reduce temperature. After about 1 minute, designs will lie flat. Remove designs from oven. Let cool.

3 Using embossing fluid and paintbrush, paint 1 side and edges of large heart. Sprinkle gold embossing powder onto heart. Using hair dryer or heat tool and following manufacturer's instructions, emboss heart. Repeat for medium heart, using silver glitter embossing powder.

4 Using swirl stamp and embossing ink pad, stamp 1 swirl on large heart. Sprinkle green embossing powder onto stamped swirl. Referring to Step 3, emboss swirl. Repeat to stamp and to emboss more swirls in desired colors on large and medium hearts.

5 Thread 3 beads onto ½" jump ring, using pliers. Connect large and medium hearts with jump ring. Add ¼" jump ring to top of large heart. Tie center of ribbon to jump ring. Knot ribbon 2" above large heart on each side. Add 3 beads to each side. Knot each length after last bead. Tie ribbon ends in bow to complete necklace.

Directions for earrings

1 Transfer 4 small hearts to Shrink-It. Cut out designs. Punch holes at top center of 2 hearts and at top and bottom of remaining hearts. Refer to steps 2 and 3 of directions for necklace, using gold embossing powder only.

2 Using embossing pen, copy swirl stamp and draw tiny swirl on 1 heart. Sprinkle green embossing powder over drawn swirl. Referring to Step 3 for necklace, emboss swirl. Repeat to draw and emboss swirls on all 4 hearts, using red, black, and silver glitter embossing powders.

3 Add 1 (¼") jump ring each to top of heart. Thread 3 beads each onto ½" jump rings, using pliers. Referring to photo, connect 2 hearts with ½" jump rings. Repeat with remaining earring. Add 1 fishhook earring to each ¼" jump ring.

Directions for jewelry box

1 Apply 2 coats of Black to entire surface of papier-mâché box and wooden balls, letting dry between coats.

2 Refer to steps 1–4 of directions for necklace, tracing 8 large hearts. Using embossing pen, draw confetti loops between swirls on each heart. Sprinkle silver glitter embossing powder over drawn loops and swirls. Refer to Step 3 of directions for necklace to emboss loops and swirls.

3 Using star stamp and embossing ink pad and referring to Step 4 for necklace, stamp and emboss stars with gold embossing powder. Stamp stars onto lid and sides of box and onto wooden balls. Finish sides of box, using swirl stamp and embossing ink pad and referring to Step 4 of directions for necklace. Add dots and confetti swirls, using same embossing methods as described in Step 2 of directions for earrings.

4 Using embossing fluid and paintbrush, paint sides of lid. Sprinkle gold embossing powder on side of lid, using same embossing methods as described in Step 3 of directions for necklace.

5 Hot-glue 1 wooden ball to center of lid. Hot-glue 1 wooden ball each to corners of box bottom. Hot-glue hearts to lid and sides of box.

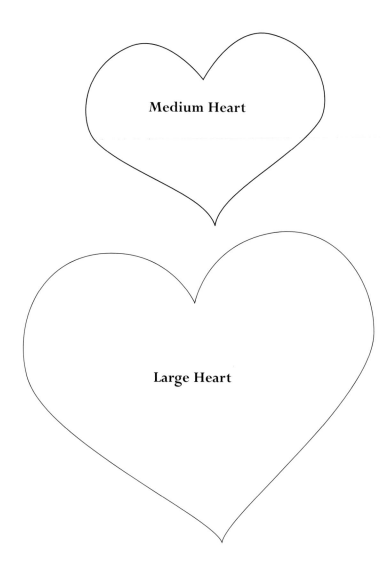

Medium Heart

Large Heart

Small Heart

Sunflower Fashions

Bright sunflowers stamped on blue denim make a playful summertime outfit.

❧ Materials ❧

Purchased overalls or denim dress
Cardboard covered with waxed paper
Fun Foam
Craft knife
Foam-core board
Aleene's Designer Tacky Glue™
Aleene's Premium-Coat™ Acrylic Paints: True
    Orange, True Yellow, Deep Beige, Deep Sage
Aleene's Premium-Coat Enhancers™: Textile
    Medium
Waxed paper
Dimensional fabric paints: gold, yellow, copper,
    dark green

Directions

Note: **For overalls,** use True Orange with
Sunflower Petal 1. **For dress,** alternate True
Orange and True Yellow with Sunflower Petals
1 and 2.

1 **For each,** wash and dry garment; do not use
fabric softener in washer or dryer. Place cardboard covered with waxed paper inside garment.

2 Transfer patterns to Fun Foam and cut out with
craft knife. Cut foam core into squares ½" larger than pattern pieces. Center and glue each foam
cutout on corresponding foam core squares.

3 Pour separate small puddles of acrylic paints
onto waxed paper. For each color of paint, mix
equal parts textile medium and paint. Referring to
photo, dip each stamp into paint and press onto garment. Repeat as desired. Let dry. To apply different
color of paint to stamp, let paint on stamp dry and
dip stamp into new color. Outline sunflower with
coordinating dimensional paint. Let dry.

4 Do not wash garment for at least 1 week. Turn
garment wrong side out, wash by hand, and
hang to dry.

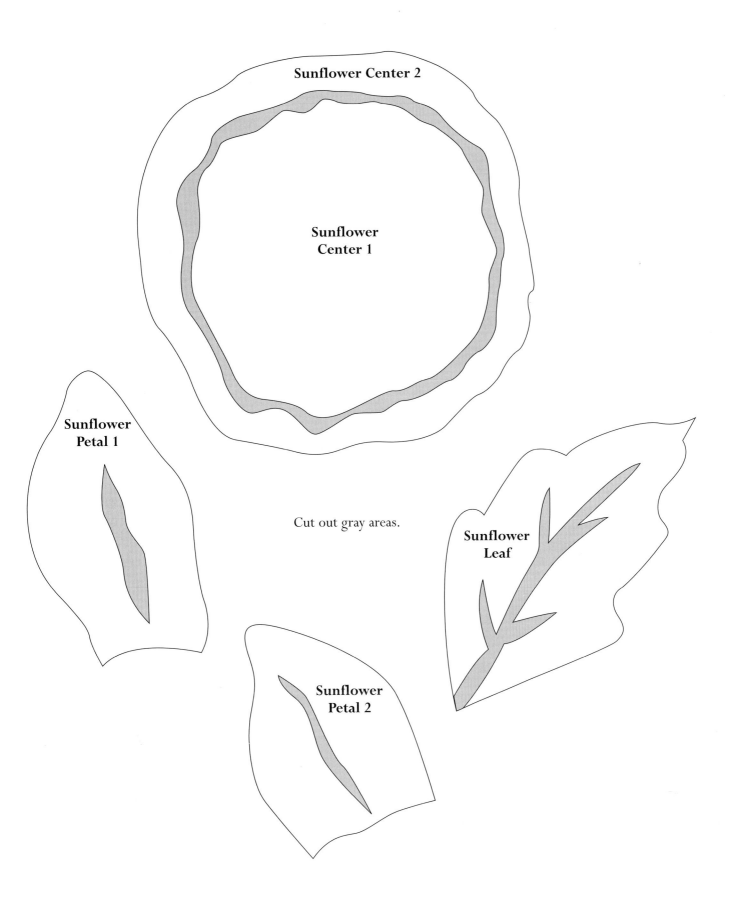

Sunflower Center 2

Sunflower
Center 1

Sunflower
Petal 1

Cut out gray areas.

Sunflower
Leaf

Sunflower
Petal 2

Flowery Monograms

Personalize a purchased shirt or scarf with a romantic hand-painted monogram. You'll be amazed at how easy the process is.

❧ Materials ❧

Blouse, scarf, or other desired garment
Cardboard covered with waxed paper
Letter stencils in desired size
Fun Foam scrap
Foam-core board scrap
Aleene's Designer Tacky Glue™
Aleene's Premium-Coat™ Acrylic Paint in desired
    colors
Aleene's Enhancers™ Textile Medium
Aleene's Premium Designer Brushes™: shader, liner
Pencil eraser or cotton swab

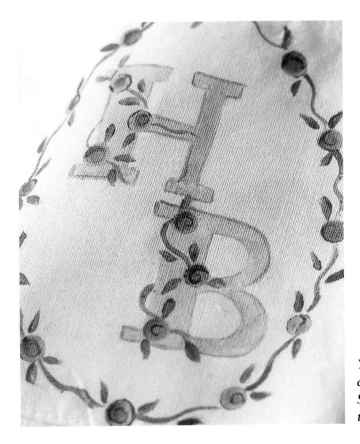

Directions

1 Wash and dry garment; do not use fabric softener in washer or dryer. Place cardboard covered with waxed paper inside garment. Using stencils, transfer desired letters for monogram to Fun Foam and cut out. Arrange letters right side down on foam-core board to form desired monogram. (Letter must be reversed when glued to read correctly after stamping.) Glue letters to foam core. Let dry. Trim excess foam core, leaving at least ½" margin all around monogram.

2 Mix equal parts of textile medium and each desired color of paint. Paint oval on garment with desired color, making sure oval is large enough for background of desired monogram. Let dry.

3 Brush even coat of desired color of paint on foam stamp. Position stamp on garment and press firmly, being sure all areas of stamp come in contact with garment. Carefully lift stamp off garment. Let dry.

4 Referring to photo, paint flowers, leaves, and vines on garment to embellish monogram and garment as desired. To paint flowers, dip pencil eraser or cotton swab into paint and press onto garment in desired position. Use liner brush to paint leaves and vines. Let dry.

5 Do not wash garment for at least 1 week. Turn garment wrong side out, wash by hand, and hang to dry.

You don't have to be a professional artist to create these beautifully embellished garments. Simply stamp letters on ready-made items and then paint them with stylized flowers and vines.

Ribbon Rose Accents

Richly colored ribbon flowers glamorize this purchased sweater. Make a gold mesh purse with more posies to complete an evening ensemble.

༂ Materials ༂

For each: Wire-edged ribbon in assorted widths and colors (See below.)

Thread to match ribbons

Aleene's Designer Tacky Glue™

Assorted beads

For sweater decoration: White fabric scrap

Aleene's Tack-It Over & Over Glue™

Purchased sweater

For purse: 1 (10¾" x 16") piece gold mesh fabric

⅛"-wide silk ribbon: 2 (8") and 1 (36") lengths pink, 1 (36") length purple

40" length gold cording

1 (8" x 9¾") piece light pink sheer fabric

Directions for sweater decoration

1 **For large rose,** cut 1 (60") length of 1½"-wide wire-edged ribbon. Fold 1 end of ribbon as shown in Diagram 1. Roll folded end of ribbon to form center of rose; stitch rolled ribbon together at bottom to secure (see Diagram 2). Pull wire at free ribbon end to gather bottom edge of ribbon and to shape rose. To secure rose, apply Designer Tacky Glue to bottom of rose while gathering. Let dry. Trim excess wire. Cut off bottom of rose below stitched line to flatten. Make 1.

2 **For medium rose,** cut 1 (36") length of 1"-wide wire-edged ribbon. Referring to large rose directions and diagrams 1 and 2, make 1 medium rose.

3 **For each large blossom,** cut 1 (7") length of 1"-wide wire-edged ribbon. Referring to Diagram 3, pull to remove wire along 1 edge of ribbon; run gathering thread along edge of ribbon without wire. Pull thread to gather ribbon into circle. Secure thread. Shape blossom as desired. Stitch beads in center of blossom as desired. Make 2.

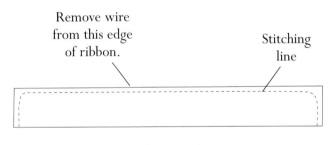

Remove wire from this edge of ribbon.

Stitching line

Diagram 3

4 **For each small blossom,** cut 1 (5") length of ½"-wide wire-edged ribbon. Referring to large blossom directions and Diagram 3, make 4 small blossoms.

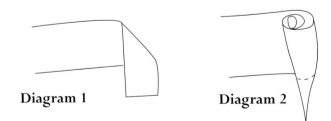

Diagram 1

Diagram 2

5 **For each large leaf,** cut 1 (8") length of 1¼"-wide wire-edged ribbon. Referring to Diagram 4, fold ribbon length in half widthwise. Fold 2 top corners down at right angle (see Diagram 5). Run gathering thread along top edge of ribbon as shown in Diagram 6. Pull thread to slightly gather ribbon. Secure thread. Open unstitched edge of ribbon and shape leaf as desired. Make 2.

6 **For each small leaf,** cut 1 (6") length of ⅝"-wide ribbon. Referring to large leaf directions and diagrams 4–6, make 3 small leaves.

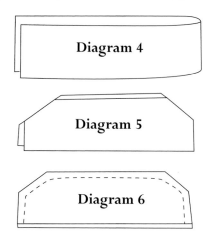

7 **To complete decoration,** arrange leaves, blossoms, and roses on fabric scrap as desired. Glue leaves and flowers to fabric, using Designer Tacky Glue. Let dry. Trim excess fabric from arrangement. Apply even coat of Tack-It Over &

Over Glue to back of fabric. Let dry for 24 to 36 hours. (Glue must be completely dry before proceeding. Glue will be sticky when dry.) When glue is completely dry, press decoration onto sweater in desired position. Remove decoration before laundering sweater. If Tack-It Over & Over Glue begins to lose its tackiness, apply new coat to back of decoration and let dry as before.

Directions for purse

1 Fold gold mesh in half widthwise. Overlap side edges and glue to make purse, leaving top open. Let dry.

2 Weave 1 (8") pink silk ribbon length through mesh at each glued edge of purse. Weave remaining pink silk ribbon through mesh along top edge of purse. Tie ribbon ends in bow at front of purse. Weave purple silk ribbon through mesh about 1" below pink ribbon (see photo). Tie ribbon ends in bow at front of purse.

3 Glue 1 end of cording inside purse at each side. Fold sheer fabric in half. Slip folded fabric inside purse for liner, gluing liner to purse around top edge. Let dry.

4 Referring to directions for sweater decoration, make 1 medium rose, 2 large blossoms, and 2 large leaves. Referring to photo on page 90, glue leaves, blossoms, and rose to front of purse as desired. Let dry.

Using variegated wire-edged ribbon, or wire-edged ribbon that is different colors on each side, will give your roses more depth and interest.

Flower-Stamped Dress

Give a plain knit dress a bit of flower power! Heidi's stamp designs make painting the flowers and the leaves a breeze. For a finishing touch, stitch coordinating buttons to the sleeves of an underlying T-shirt.

❧ Materials ❧

For each: Fun Foam: 1 (5½" x 6¼") piece, scraps
Foam-core board
Aleene's Designer Tacky Glue™
Cardboard covered with waxed paper
Aleene's Premium-Coat™ Acrylic Paints: Medium Turquoise, White, True Apricot, Medium Green, Deep Green
Aleene's Enhancers™ Textile Medium
Sponge paintbrush
Purple dimensional fabric paint
For dress: Purchased plain knit dress
For T-shirt: Purchased plain T-shirt
Embroidery needle
Embroidery floss in colors to coordinate with buttons
Variety bright-colored buttons

Directions

1 **For each,** wash and dry garments; do not use fabric softener in washer or dryer.

2 To make stamps, transfer flower, flower center, and leaf patterns to Fun Foam scraps and cut out. Cut foam core into pieces ½" larger all around than pattern pieces; also cut 1 (6" x 6½") piece of foam core. Center and glue 5½" x 6¼" piece of Fun Foam on 6" x 6½" piece of foam core. Center

and glue remaining Fun Foam cutouts on corresponding foam-core pieces, leaving space between flower Fun Foam pieces as indicated on pattern.

3 **For dress,** insert cardboard covered with waxed paper inside dress. For each color of acrylic paint, mix equal parts textile medium and paint. Paint rectangular foam stamp with Medium Turquoise. Referring to photo, position stamp on front of dress and press firmly, being sure all areas of stamp come in contact with printing surface. (Practice on scrap paper to determine correct amount of pressure and paint needed to get desired effect.) Let dry. Repeat to stamp flower with White, flower center with True Apricot, and leaves with Medium Green and Deep Green, letting paint dry before stamping next shape. Using purple dimensional paint and referring to photo, paint swirls. Let dry.

4 Do not wash garment for at least 1 week. Turn garment wrong side out, wash by hand, and hang to dry.

5 **For T-shirt,** fold hem of each sleeve up twice. Use embroidery needle and embroidery floss to slipstitch hems in place and to stitch buttons around turned-up sleeve hems.

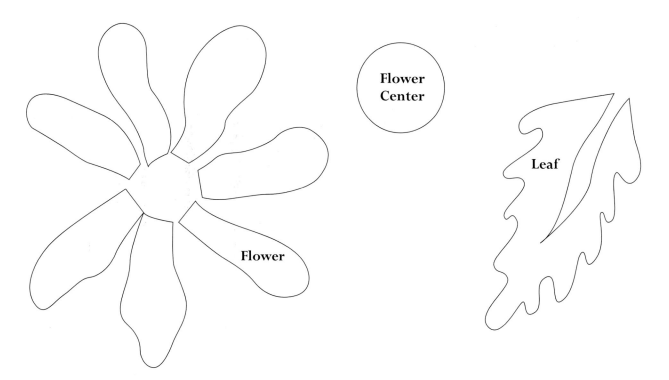

Flower Center

Leaf

Flower

Dangling Darlings

Cut, color, and shrink boy and girl charms to make a necklace or a pin.
Glue an acrylic jewel to each charm to represent a child's birthstone.

❧ Materials ❧

For each: Aleene's Opake Shrink-It™ Plastic
Fine-grade sandpaper
Fine-tip permanent black marker
Colored pencils
Aleene's Baking Board or nonstick cookie sheet, sprinkled with baby powder
Aleene's Designer Tacky Glue™
Assorted colors 5-mm round flat-backed acrylic jewels
For necklace: ¼"-diameter hole punch
Silver jewelry findings: 8-mm jump rings, 7-mm round spacer beads, pony beads, desired length ball chain with clasp
Needlenose pliers
For pin: pin back

Directions for necklace

1 Sand 1 side of Shrink-It so that markings will adhere. Be sure to thoroughly sand both vertically and horizontally. Using marker, trace desired number of child charms, including hanger loop at top of each charm, onto sanded side of Shrink-It. (Marker ink may run on sanded surface; runs will shrink and disappear.) Use colored pencils to color each design. (Colors will be more intense after shrinking.) Cut out each design. Punch 1 hole in each charm where indicated on pattern.

2 Preheat toaster oven or conventional oven to 275° to 300°. Place each design on room-temperature baking board and bake in oven. Edges should begin to curl within 25 seconds; if not, increase temperature slightly. If edges begin to curl as soon as designs are put in oven, reduce temperature. After about 1 minute, designs will lie flat. Remove from oven. Let cool.

3 Glue 1 jewel to each charm. Let dry. Attach 1 jump ring to hanger loop of each charm, using pliers. Thread charms, spacer beads, and pony beads onto ball chain in desired order.

Directions for pin

1 Referring to Step 1 of directions for necklace, trace hearts pattern and 3 child charms onto sanded side of Shrink-It, omitting hanger loop at top of each charm. Use colored pencils to color each design. Cut out each design. Refer to Step 2 of directions for necklace to shrink each design.

2 Glue 1 jewel to each charm. Let dry. Glue charms in place on hearts (see photo). Let dry. Glue pin back to back of design. Let dry.

This playful pin would also make a darling barrette.

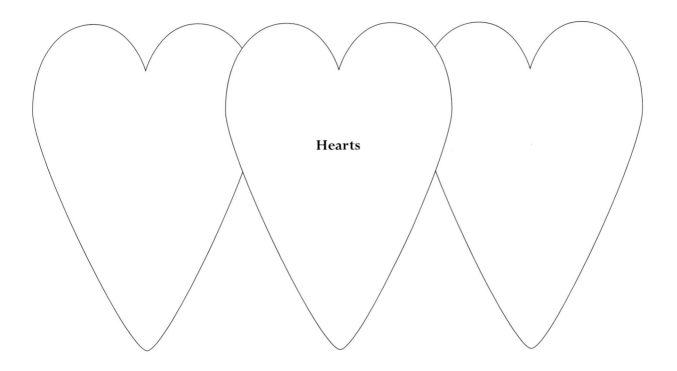

Hearts

Hole

Girl

Hole

Boy

Victorian Vest

She'll be the picture of femininity in this lace-trimmed vest. Touches of hand embroidery, ribbon roses, and elegant buttons complete the vintage look.

Materials

Purchased plain natural-colored vest
Assorted beige crocheted laces and doilies
White-on-white fabric scraps
Aleene's OK to Wash-It™ Glue
Aleene's Fusible Web™
Embroidery needle and white embroidery floss
Assorted beige and white buttons
Assorted beads
Beige satin ribbon roses

Directions

1 Wash, dry, and press vest, laces, doilies, and fabric scraps.

2 Referring to photo, glue crocheted laces and doilies to front of vest as desired. Let dry.

3 Fuse web to wrong side of fabric scraps. Transfer heart patterns to paper side of fabric scraps as desired. Cut out heart shapes. Remove paper backing. Fuse hearts as desired to vest front. Using embroidery needle and floss, buttonhole-stitch around edges of fabric hearts.

4 Glue buttons, beads, and ribbon roses to front of vest as desired. Let dry.

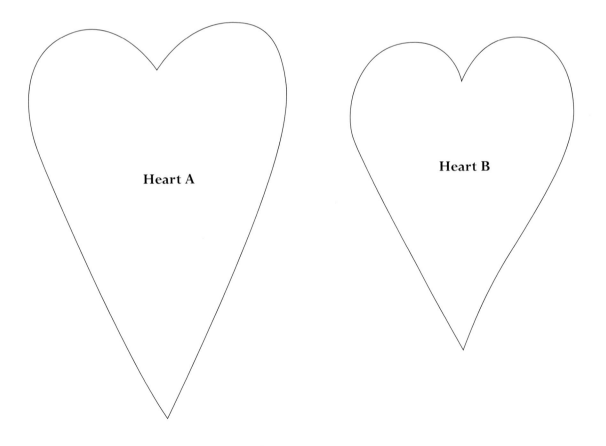

Heart A

Heart B

Herb Jacket

A perfect smock for puttering around in the garden, this top is also a great lightweight jacket for cool spring days.

🐦 Materials 🐦

White cotton button-front jacket
Cardboard covered with waxed paper
Aleene's Premium-Coat™ Acrylic Paints: Light
    Yellow, Soft Sage, Deep Beige, Soft Sand, True
    Fuchsia, Dusty Sage, Deep Sage, Dusty Violet,
    Deep Green, Dusty Khaki
Aleene's Enhancers™ Textile Medium
Paper plates
Small paint roller
Brushes: large, stencil
Pop-up craft sponges
Cotton swabs
2" letter stencils
Paper cup
Dimensional fabric paints: lavender, dark green,
    bronze, brown

Directions

1 Wash and dry jacket; do not use fabric softener in washer or dryer.

2 Insert cardboard covered with waxed paper inside jacket sleeves and body. For each color of acrylic paint, mix equal parts textile medium and paint on paper plate. Referring to photo and using paint roller and large paintbrush, randomly paint background blocks of color on jacket with Light Yellow and Soft Sage. Let dry.

3 Transfer patterns to pop-up sponges and cut out. Dip sponge shapes into water and wring out excess water.

4 Dip flower center sponge into Deep Beige; sponge-paint centers on jacket. Let dry. Dip cotton swab into Soft Sand; then dab circles on centers. Let dry. Dip flower petal sponge into True Fuchsia; bending sponge to create different shapes, sponge-paint petals. Let dry. Dip large leaf sponge into Dusty Sage and then into Deep Sage; sponge-paint leaves below flowers. Let dry.

5 Dip bay leaf sponge into Dusty Sage and then into Deep Sage; sponge-paint bay leaves. Let dry. Dip sage leaf sponge into Dusty Sage and then into Deep Sage; sponge-paint sage leaves. Let dry. Dip cotton swab into Dusty Violet and use cotton swab to create sage leaf blossoms. Let dry.

6 Using letter stencils, stencil brush, and Deep Green, stencil "HERBS" on jacket. Let dry. Dip bottom of paper cup into Dusty Khaki and stamp circles for seed packets. Use sage leaf sponge dipped into Deep Green and cotton swab dipped into Dusty Violet to paint flowers in seed packet circles. Let dry.

7 Use lavender dimensional paint to paint "SEEDS" on packets. While paint is still wet, cover with paper towel and press gently to flatten paint. Let dry. Repeat process, using dark green dimensional paint to paint herbs, "SAGE," and stems on flowers, sage, and bay. Let dry. Repeat, using bronze dimensional paint to paint rosemary stems and "BAY." Let dry. Repeat, using brown dimensional paint to paint "ROSEMARY." Let dry.

8 Do not wash garment for at least 1 week. Turn garment wrong side out, wash by hand, and hang to dry.

Sage Leaf

Bay Leaf

Flower Center

Large Leaf

Flower Petal

Everyday Pleasures

Page 134

Page 106

Throughout these pages you will find that simple pleasures are priceless treasures. Discover lots of little ways to show someone how much you think of her. From unusual candles to pretty packages to invigorating body splashes—they're all featured here.

Page 108

Stained-glass Frame

Add a border of bright flowers to a large acrylic box frame to complement a favorite photo.

Materials

Aleene's Tissue Paper™: dark purple, pink, orange, yellow, dark green, light green, light blue
1 (11" x 14") acrylic box frame
Aleene's Reverse Collage™ Glue
Sponge paintbrush
Aleene's 3-D Foiling™ Glue
Aleene's Gold Crafting Foil™

Directions

1 Referring to photo for inspiration, transfer patterns to tissue paper and cut out desired number of flowers and leaves. (Center and draw 5" x 7" rectangle on paper insert from frame. Arrange flowers and leaves on paper around rectangle to determine desired placement and number of cutouts needed.) Working over small area at a time, brush coat of Reverse Collage Glue on inside of acrylic frame where cutouts will be placed. Press 1 cutout into glue-covered area. Brush coat of Reverse

Collage Glue on top of cutout, pressing out any air bubbles. Repeat to glue remaining cutouts to frame, leaving space for photo in center of frame. Let dry.

2 Cut or tear odd-shaped pieces of light blue tissue paper for background areas of frame. (Do not apply tissue paper to area where photo will be placed.) Crumple each paper piece and then flatten, leaving some wrinkles. In same manner as before, glue light blue paper pieces on inside of frame to cover background of floral design, using Reverse Collage Glue. Let dry.

3 Apply lines of 3-D Foiling Glue to right side of frame, outlining flowers and leaves and adding details to designs. Let dry. (Glue will be opaque and sticky when dry. Glue must be thoroughly dry before foil is applied.) To apply foil, lay foil dull side down on top of glue lines. Using finger, gently but firmly press foil onto glue, completely covering glue with foil. Peel away foil paper. Assemble frame.

Flower A

Flower C

Leaf A

Flower B

Leaf B

Leaf C

Flower D

Doily Delights

Shimmering metallic doilies dress your gifts in style.
A snip of the scissors and a few quick folds are all it takes to create
the angel or fan toppers shown here.

❧ Materials ❧

For each: Aleene's Tacky Glue™

For angel topper: Paper doilies: 1 (6"-diameter) gold metallic, 1 (8") square white, 1 (6"-diameter) silver metallic

Spray adhesive

Wrapped gift (See Note.)

Ribbons: 36" length 1"-wide sheer dark green (or length needed to fit around gift; see Step 3), 4" length 1/8"-wide pink silk

3/4"-diameter white button

Artificial gold wedding ring

For fan topper: 1 (6"-diameter) silver metallic paper doily

Ribbons: 1 (36") length dark pink and 2 (2") lengths green 1"-wide wire-edged, 36" length 1"-wide sheer purple (or length needed to fit around gift; see Step 3)

Wrapped gift (See Note.)

Note: Heidi glued assorted white doilies onto gift boxes for wrapped gifts shown in photo.

Directions for angel topper

1 Cut gold paper doily in half. For angel's dress, fanfold 1 doily half to make 1/4"-deep pleats so that curved edge of doily is bottom of dress (Diagram 1). Glue pleats together at straight edge of doily half, using Tacky Glue. Let dry.

2 For wings, cut remaining gold doily half into wedge-shaped quarters. Set 2 quarters aside for another use.

3 Referring to photo and using spray adhesive, center and glue white doily on top of wrapped gift; glue silver doily on top of white doily. Then glue wings on top of silver doily. Let dry. Wrap dark green ribbon around gift and tie ends in bow on top of gift, arranging bow on top of doily wings. Referring to photo, glue angel's dress, button for head, and wedding ring for halo on top of bow, using Tacky Glue. Tie pink silk ribbon in bow and glue to angel at neck. Let dry.

Directions for fan topper

1 Cut silver doily in half. Fanfold each doily half to make 1/2"-wide pleats so that curved edge of doily is bottom of fan (Diagram 2). Glue pleats together at straight edge of doily. Let dry.

2 Referring to medium rose directions given for Ribbon Rose Accents on page 91, make 1 medium rose with dark pink ribbon. For each leaf, fold down 1 end of 2" green ribbon to form right angle (Diagram 3) and then fold left end of ribbon to back along line indicated to form point (Diagram 4). Pinch ribbon ends together to shape bottom of leaf (Diagram 5).

3 Wrap purple ribbon around gift and tie ends in bow on top of gift. Glue 1 fan on each side of bow, with glued ends of fans butted. Glue leaves and rose on top of glued ends of fans. Let dry.

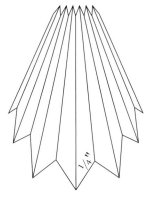

Diagram 1

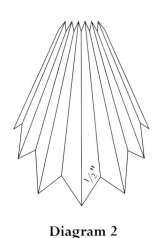

Diagram 2

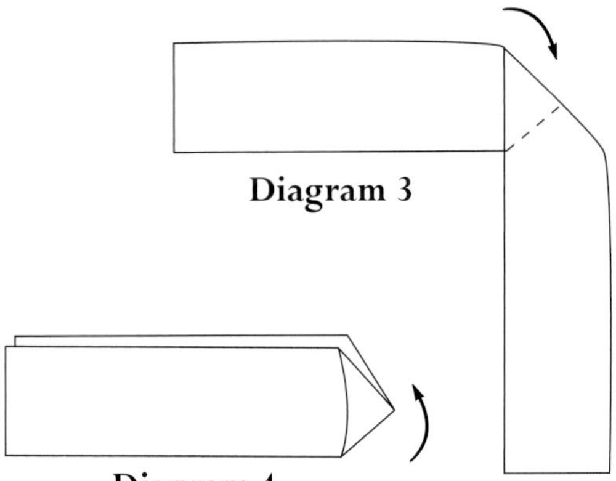

Diagram 3

Diagram 4

Diagram 5

Body Splash

Try your hand at making scented body splash. The following recipe requires no exotic ingredients or complicated instructions.

Materials

8 ounces distilled water
Essential oil
Essential color
Clean, dry bottle with cork
Aleene's Ultimate Glue Gun™
Aleene's All-Purpose Glue Sticks™
Ribbon (optional)
Seashells (optional)

Directions

Mix distilled water, 2 drops of essential oil, and 2 drops of essential color. Pour into bottle. Seal with cork. Hot-glue ribbon and seashells onto bottle as desired.

Merry Message Board

Not only is this tea-rrific board handy for jotting down important messages, but it also adds a whimsical accent to a breakfast nook or a kitchen.

❧ Materials for tea board ❧

Sponge paintbrush
1 (8½" x 11½") purchased chalk board with
    wooden frame
Aleene's Premium-Coat™ Acrylic Paints: Light
    Green, True Fuchsia, Light Fuchsia, Deep Violet
Aleene's Premium Designer Brush™: shader
Waxed paper
Fun Foam: pink, purple, blue, green
Posterboard scrap
Aleene's Tacky Glue™
Dimensional paints: pearlescent fuchsia, pearlescent
    purple, green
Drill with ¹⁄₁₆" bit
1 (24") length 18-gauge wire
Aleene's Satin Sheen Twisted Ribbon™: beige

Directions for tea board

1 Using sponge brush, paint wooden frame of
chalk board Light Green. Let dry. Referring to
photo and using shader brush and True Fuchsia,
paint hearts around frame. Let dry.

2 Pour separate puddles of Light Fuchsia and
Deep Violet onto waxed paper. Dip tip of shader
brush handle into Light Fuchsia and then dot paint
around edges of each heart. Wipe off handle of
brush. Dip tip of brush handle into Deep Violet and
dot paint in waves between hearts. Let dry.

3 Transfer teacup handle and teapot handle, lid,
spout, and base patterns to pink Fun Foam; pot
and teacup rim patterns to purple; cup pattern to
blue; and teacup saucer pattern to green. Cut out
shapes. For base, transfer teapot outline and teacup-
and-saucer outline to posterboard scrap. Cut out
shapes.

4 Referring to photo, glue teapot foam shapes in
place on posterboard teapot base and teacup-
and-saucer foam shapes in place on corresponding
posterboard base. Let dry. Referring to photo and
using dimensional paints, embellish teapot, teacup,
and saucer. Let dry. Glue teapot to upper left corner
of message board. Glue teacup with saucer to lower
right corner of message board. Let dry.

5 Drill 2 holes, 2½" from side edges, in top front
edge of message board. For hanger, twist wire
around pencil. Pull wire to stretch coils slightly.
Working from front, insert 1" of wire ends into
holes. Bend wire ends up. Tear twisted ribbon into
strips. Holding several torn strips together, tie ribbon strips in bow at top of wire hanger.

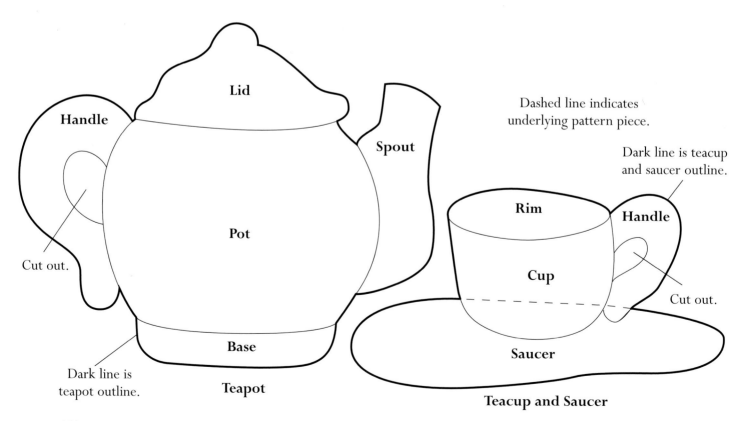

Handle

Lid

Spout

Cut out.

Pot

Dashed line indicates
underlying pattern piece.

Dark line is teacup
and saucer outline.

Rim   Handle

Cup

Cut out.

Base

Dark line is
teapot outline.

Saucer

Teapot

Teacup and Saucer

❧ Materials for rose board ❧

Sponge paintbrush
1 (8½" x 11½") purchased chalk board with
    wooden frame
Aleene's Premium-Coat™ Acrylic Paints: Light
    Lavender, Light Fuchsia, Medium Fuchsia, Soft
    Sage, Deep Sage, Deep Beige, Light Yellow
Pop-up craft sponge
Waxed paper
Paper towel
Aleene's Premium Designer Brush™: liner
Fine-tip permanent black marker
1 (38") length 1¼"-wide lace
1 (24") length ¼"-wide fuchsia satin ribbon

Directions for rose board

1 Using sponge brush, paint wooden frame Light
  Lavender. Let dry.

2 Cut ¾"-diameter wavy circle and ¾"-long leaf
  shape from pop-up craft sponge. Wet sponge
shapes and ring out excess water. Pour separate puddles of Light Fuchsia and Medium Fuchsia onto
waxed paper. Dip wavy circle sponge into each

color, blotting excess paint on paper towel.
Referring to photo, sponge-paint roses around edges
of wooden frame. Let dry. In same manner, sponge-
paint leaves between roses, using leaf-shaped
sponge, Soft Sage, and Deep Sage. Let dry.

3 Using liner brush and Medium Fuchsia, outline
  roses and paint swirls in centers of roses. Let
dry. Using liner brush, Deep Beige, and Soft Sage,
paint veins in leaves and vines connecting leaves. Let
dry. Pour puddle of Light Yellow onto waxed paper.
Dip tip of liner brush handle into paint. Referring
to photo, dot Light Yellow accent flowers between
roses. Let dry.

4 Using liner brush and Medium Fuchsia, paint
  "Messages" at top of board. Let dry. Using permanent marker, trace over painted word (see
photo).

5 Referring to photo, glue finished edge of lace to
  back of wooden frame along edges. Let dry. Cut
satin ribbon in half. For hanger, glue 1 cut end of
each ribbon length to back of message board at each
upper corner. Let dry. Tie ends of ribbon in bow.

*If you prefer a lacy,
daintier style, create
our rose board.*

Dragonfly Table Decor

Give this tableware holder and dragonfly napkin rings as a hostess gift to help prepare for a picnic or an outdoor buffet.

Materials

For each: Aleene's Designer Tacky Glue™
Assorted colors Fun Foam
For holder: empty 87-ounce laundry detergent
   box
Craft knife
Batting
Fabrics: 1½ yards 36"-wide dragonfly print,
   1 (1¼" x 18") torn strip purple print
2 (5¼" x 7") pieces medium-weight cardboard
Assorted colors Aleene's Premium-Coat™ Acrylic
   Paint
Fine-tip paintbrush
For 1 napkin ring: Clothespin
Assorted colors dimensional paint

Directions for holder

1 Cut lid from box, using craft knife. Set lid aside for another use. Wrap and glue batting to cover sides of box. Cut 1 (30" x 36") piece, 1 (5½" x 8¾") piece, 1 (12" x 16") piece, and 1 (3¼" x 34") strip from dragonfly fabric. Turn under and glue 1" along 1 (30") edge of 30" x 36" fabric for hem. With 8" of fabric extending beyond top edge of box, wrap and glue fabric around box to cover sides, overlapping 30" edges and placing hemmed edge on top. Fold and glue excess fabric at top of box to inside; fold excess fabric at bottom of box as if wrapping a package. Let dry.

2 Glue 5½" x 8¾" fabric inside bottom of box. Stack cardboard pieces and, with edges aligned, glue pieces together. Wrap and glue 12" x 16" piece of fabric to cover cardboard. Let dry. Glue fabric-covered cardboard inside box to divide box into 2 equal compartments. Turn under and glue 1" along each long edge of 3¼" x 34" strip to make strip 1¼" wide. Let dry.

3 With ends butted at center bottom of box, glue 1¼"-wide strip to bottom and sides of box for handle. Tie purple fabric strip in bow. Glue bow to 1 side of box at handle (see photo). Let dry.

4 Transfer patterns to desired colors of Fun Foam and cut 2 small bodies, 4 wing As, and 4 wing Bs. Referring to photo, glue foam pieces to side of box to form 2 dragonflies. Paint antennae and dots on wings with acrylic paints. Let dry.

Directions for 1 napkin ring

Cut 1 (1⅝" x 7½") strip from desired color of Fun Foam. Curve strip into circle, overlapping ends 1", and glue. Use clothespin to hold ends together until glue is dry. Transfer patterns to desired colors of Fun Foam and cut 1 large body, 2 wing Cs, and 2 wing Ds. Referring to photo, glue body and wings on ring to form dragonfly. Use clothespin to hold pieces in place until glue is dry. Paint details on body and wings with dimensional paints. Let dry.

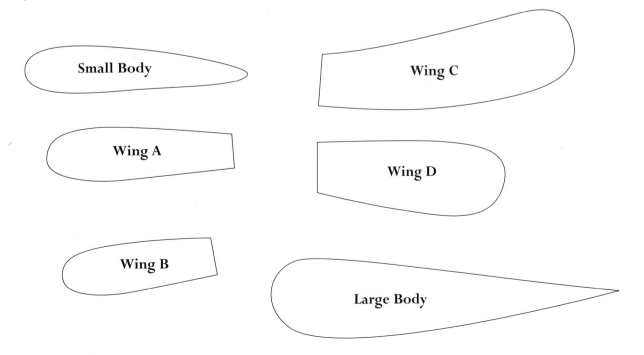

Small Body

Wing C

Wing A

Wing D

Wing B

Large Body

Handmade Paper Boxes

Handmade papers are the secret to these extraordinary gift boxes. Flower petals and potpourri add color, texture, and aroma to the paper. For paper with a woody texture, substitute pencil shavings.

✎ Materials ✎
(for handmade paper)
2 (8" x 10") wooden picture frames
1 (8½" x 10½") piece window screen
Heavy-duty stapler
Aleene's Cotton Linter Paper™
White paper towels (generic brand works best) or
    white construction paper
Blender
Fresh flowers and leaves torn into bits
Plastic dishpan (slightly larger than picture frames)
Newspapers
Terry towel
1 (9" x 11") piece white felt
Clean kitchen sponge

Directions for handmade paper

1 Remove glass and backing from each frame and set aside for another use. Stretch window screen over 1 frame and staple in place to make mold. Frame without screen is called deckle.

2 Tear cotton linter paper and 1 or 2 paper towels into 1" pieces. Put paper pieces into container of blender. Add water to top line of blender. Let stand for several hours or overnight to let paper dissolve. Blend pulp, stopping often to check consistency, until paper is mostly dissolved but not lumpy. Put bits of flowers and leaves into container of blender and blend to mix.

3 Fill plastic dishpan halfway with lukewarm water. Pour blended pulp into dishpan. Stir to suspend pulp in water. With edges aligned and screen side up, place deckle on top of mold. Dip deckle and mold into dishpan and completely cover screen with even layer of pulp. Slowly lift deckle and mold above water and allow excess water to drain from pulp (see Photo A). Remove deckle and mold from dishpan. Carefully lift deckle off mold and set aside.

Photo B: Sponging water from back of screen

Photo A: Draining excess water from pulp

4 To prepare drying surface, stack newspapers (about 1" thick), towel, and felt on flat surface. Turn mold over, with pulp on felt. To remove mold from paper, gently sponge excess water from back of screen (see Photo B). Paper will release from screen when enough moisture has been sponged away. Remove mold and set aside. Let paper dry overnight. (Depending on humidity, paper may take longer to dry.) When paper is dry enough to hold together, remove from drying surface and set aside to dry completely.

❧ Materials ❧
(for each gift box)
Aleene's BoxMaker™ and BoxBlanks™
2 (8" x 10") pieces handmade paper
Assorted dried or silk flowers and leaves
Aleene's Designer Tacky Glue™
Raffia or thin ribbon (optional)

Directions for gift box

1 Cut box blank and 1 sheet of paper to desired size for box. For 4" x 6" x 2" box, use 1 (8" x 10") piece of box blank for box bottom and 2 (8" x 10") pieces of paper. For 2" x 5" x 2" box, use 1 (6" x 9") piece of box blank for box bottom and 2 (6" x 9") pieces of paper.

2 Following BoxMaker directions, adhere 1 piece of handmade paper to right side of box blank for box bottom. Referring to BoxMaker directions, make box bottom with paper-covered box blank and make box top with remaining sheet of paper.

3 Glue assorted dried or silk flowers and leaves to box top. Let dry. If desired, tie raffia or ribbon in bow and glue to box top. Let dry.

Tea & Coffee Boxes

Whatever her beverage of choice, one of these boxes is sure to please. For an added treat, fill the box with her favorite specialty coffees or teas.

Materials
(for 1 box)
Wooden wine box (See Note.)
Aleene's Premium-Coat™ Acrylic Paint: Ivory or Beige
Aleene's Premium Designer Brush™
2" letter stencils
Aleene's Tissue Paper™: ivory gingham, green gingham, blue gingham, red gingham, dark blue, tan
Aleene's Paper Napkin Appliqué™ Glue
Dimensional paints: dark blue, ivory, red, light brown

Note: Wine box made by Dufeck. To order, call Aleene's Consumer Services at (800) 825-3363.

Directions
1 **For tea box,** paint box Ivory. **For coffee box,** paint box Beige. Let dry.

2 **For each,** Referring to photo for colors, transfer pot and cup patterns and desired letter stencils to gingham tissue paper and cut out. **For tea box,** cut 65 approximately ½" squares and 12 approximately ¼" x ½" rectangles from dark blue tissue. **For coffee box,** cut same number and size of squares and rectangles from tan tissue.

3 **For each,** referring to photo and using Napkin Appliqué Glue and paintbrush, glue 11 (½") tissue paper squares along inside back of box, spacing squares evenly. Glue 2 rows of 12 tissue paper squares along top and bottom edge of lid, spacing squares evenly. Glue remaining squares along edges of front of box and ¼" x ½" rectangles along front edge of lid, spacing rectangles evenly. Referring to photo, glue pots, cups, and letters to box. Brush thin coat of Napkin Appliuqé Glue over entire box. Let dry.

4 **For tea box,** referring to photo, outline letters with dots of dark blue dimensional paint. Let dry. **For coffee box,** outline letters with dots of ivory dimensional paint. Let dry. **For each,** referring to photo, embellish squares, pots, and cups with dashes, hearts, and swirls in various colors of dimensional paint. Let dry.

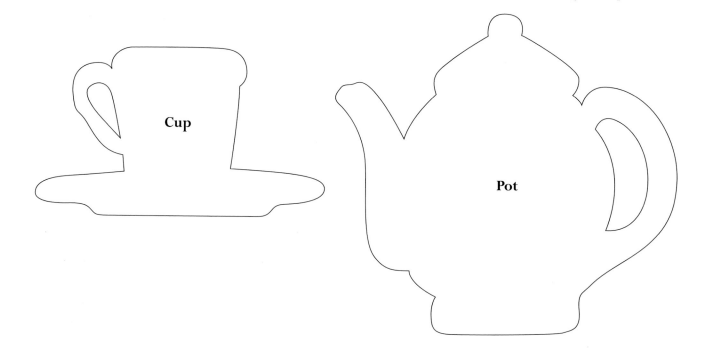

Cup

Pot

Enchanting Wind Chimes

Select a plate that is already cracked or chipped to make this project.
Mismatched spoons found at flea markets or garage sales and beads from
the crafts store complete the design.

Materials

Protective glasses
Ceramic plate
Old towel
Hammer
Wire coat hangers
Wire cutters
Pliers
6 tablespoons or soupspoons
Drill with ⅛" and ¼" bits
15" length 1½"-diameter piece driftwood or tree
    branch
Fishing line
Assorted beads in colors to match plate
25" length silver ball chain with clasp

Directions

1 Put on protective glasses. Place plate wrong side up inside folded towel and strike center bottom of plate with hammer to break plate into at least 5 pieces. After each strike, check broken pieces for desired size and shape.

2 For each plate piece, use wire cutters to cut 1 (7" to 9") length from coat hanger. Using pliers, wrap 1 wire length around each plate piece to form hanger, shaping wire into small loop at top of plate piece (see photos).

3 Working on hard protected work surface, hammer bowl of each spoon flat. Center and drill 1 (⅛") hole through handle of each spoon.

4 Drill 11 (⅛") holes side by side through center of driftwood. Also drill 2 (¼") holes about 3" apart on driftwood.

5 Cut 6 (8" to 12") lengths of fishing line. For each chimes dangle, knot spoon or wire hanger loop on plate piece to 1 end of 1 length of fishing line. Thread beads on line as desired, knotting line after last bead. If desired, knot line a few inches above previous knot and thread additional beads on line. Thread free end of line through 1 (⅛") hole in driftwood, being sure spoons and plate pieces will touch when hanging. Thread 1 bead on free end of fishing line and knot thread.

6 For chimes hanger, thread silver ball chain through ¼" holes in driftwood and connect clasp ends.

120

Everything's Rosy!

A rose by any other name makes a great gift even sweeter. Mix water with acrylic paint for the watercolor effect shown here. The dimensional gold details on each rose add richness to the cards and to the package topper.

The torn edges of the watercolor paper mimic the soft lines of the washed paints.

🐚 **Materials** 🐚

For each rose: 1 (6" x 8") piece white watercolor
    paper

Aleene's Premium-Coat™ Acrylic Paints: True Red,
    Medium Red, True Fuchsia, or Deep Fuchsia for
    rose; Deep Green or Deep Sage for leaves

Aleene's Premium Designer Brush™: shader

Aleene's 3-D Foiling Glue™

Aleene's Gold Crafting Foil™

8 (¼") squares foam-core board

Aleene's Tacky Glue™

For both cards: 2 (6⅞" x 9⅞") pieces card stock
    or purchased cards

Watercolor paper: 1 (4" x 6") torn piece light pink
    and 1 (⅞" x 2") torn piece white for rose card,
    white scrap for thank-you card

1 (4¾" x 6¾") piece tissue paper for thank-you
    card

Directions

1 **For each rose,** use pencil to lightly trace pattern for rose A or rose B onto 6" x 8" piece of watercolor paper. Use leaves on rose A as guide to add leaves to rose B, if desired. For each color of paint, mix 2 parts water with 1 part paint to make thin wash. Paint design with thinned paint, allowing paint to bleed on paper for shaded effect. Let dry.

2 Apply lines of 3-D Foiling Glue to painted paper to outline design and to add details. Let dry. (Glue will be sticky when dry. Glue must be thoroughly dry before foil is applied.) To apply gold foil, lay foil dull side down on top of glue lines. Using your finger, press foil onto glue, completely covering glue with foil. Peel away foil paper.

3 Cut or tear out rose, adding ¼" all around design. Glue 8 foam-core squares to back of rose, using Tacky Glue. Let dry. Make 1 rose for each package topper or card.

4 **For package topper,** glue 1 rose onto desired gift box, using Tacky Glue. Let dry.

For each card, fold 1 (6⅞" x 9⅞") piece of card stock in half widthwise to form card.

For rose card, center and glue 4" x 6" piece of watercolor paper on card front, using Tacky Glue. Referring to Step 1, paint ⅞" x 2" piece of watercolor paper with desired color of thinned paint. Let dry. Referring to Step 2, write "Rose" on painted paper with 3-D Foiling Glue and cover with foil.

For thank-you card, crumple tissue paper and then flatten it, leaving some wrinkles. Center and glue tissue paper on card front, using Tacky Glue sparingly. Referring to Step 2, write "Thank You" on white scrap of watercolor paper with 3-D Foiling Glue and cover with foil. Tear away excess paper, leaving about ¼" all around words.

For each card, using Tacky Glue. Glue rose and words in place on card front, using Tacky Glue. Let dry.

Rose B

Rose A

Tea for Two

A tisket, a tasket, fill up a teatime basket. Surprise a tea-loving friend with a basket filled with comforting tea and cookies.

🙠 Materials 🙠

For each: Aleene's Tacky Glue™
Aleene's Fusible Web™
For basket: White heart-shaped basket with hinged lid and handles (See Note.)
1 (12") square thin batting
1 (12") square posterboard
Fabrics: 1 (12") square, 1 (2¾" x 35") strip, and 2 (1" x 42") strips pink-and-white stripe; 1 (3" x 8½") piece blue stripe floral print; 1 (2½" x 8") piece and 4 (1" x 14") torn strips light green floral print
30" length 1"-wide white lace trim
Dimensional paints: pearlescent green, dark pink
For card: 1 (6" x 8¾") piece white paper
Fabrics: 1 (3¾" x 5½") piece pink-and-white stripe, 1 (3" x 4¼") piece green print
Craft knife
Pink ribbon rose
Tea bag
For box: Aleene's BoxMaker™ and BoxBlanks™
Fabrics: 1 (9") square and 1 (5½") square light green floral print, 1 (5¾") square pink-and-white check
1 (5½") square posterboard
Pearlescent green dimensional paint
Pink ribbon rose

Directions for basket

Note: Heidi's heart-shaped basket is 10" wide, 13" long, and 8" deep. Be sure to adjust fabric requirements as needed to fit your basket. If desired, cut and glue additional fabric pieces to cover inside of basket.

1 Using basket lid as guide, cut 1 heart each from batting and posterboard. Using posterboard heart as guide, cut 1 heart from 12" square of pink-and-white fabric, adding 1" all around. Glue batting heart to 1 side of posterboard heart. With batting side down, place posterboard heart on wrong side of fabric heart. Fold and glue excess fabric to posterboard, clipping curves as needed. Let dry. Glue bound edge of lace to wrong side of heart so that lace extends beyond heart. Let dry.

2 Fuse web to wrong side of 3" x 8½" blue stripe floral and 2½" x 8" light green floral. Transfer patterns (on page 126) to fabrics and cut 1 large teapot and 4 small teapots from blue stripe floral and 1 spout, 1 lid, 1 handle, 1 base, and 4 small teapots from light green floral. Cut out shapes.

3 Referring to photo for positioning, fuse large teapot, spout, lid, handle, and base to right side of fabric heart. Fuse small teapots to 2¾" x 35" fabric strip, spacing evenly and alternating prints.

4 Write "Tea Time" and draw tiny hearts on fabric heart with dimensional paints. Let dry. Glue heart in place on basket lid. Beginning at center back of basket, wrap and glue fused fabric strip around basket, overlapping ends, and glue. Let dry.

5 For handles, wrap 1 (42"-long) strip around each handle to cover, gluing ends to secure. Tie 1 light green floral strip around each end of each handle.

Directions for card

1 Fuse web to wrong side of fabrics. Fold paper in half widthwise to form card. Ravel edges of pink-and-white fabric. Center and fuse pink-and-white fabric on card front. Transfer pattern to green print fabric and cut 1 cup. Referring to photo for positioning, fuse cup on card front.

2 Referring to pattern and cutting through card front only, cut slit in cup. Glue ribbon rose to front of cup. Let dry. Slip tea bag into slit in card front.

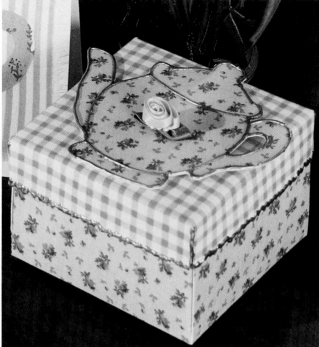

Directions for box

1 Referring to BoxMaker directions, cut box blanks to make 1 (3¾") square box and lid. Fuse 9" light green floral print square to box blank piece for box. Fuse pink-and-white check fabric to box blank piece for lid. Complete box and lid, following BoxMaker directions.

2 Transfer entire large teapot pattern to posterboard and remaining floral print fabric; cut 1 of each. Fuse fabric teapot to posterboard teapot. Outline teapot and rim of box lid and add details to teapot with dimensional paint. Let dry. Glue ribbon rose on teapot. Glue teapot on box lid. Let dry.

Lid

Handle

Large
Teapot

Cut out.

Base

Small Teapot

Cut out.

Slit

Cup

Friendship Treasures Heart Box

Celebrate friendship with this gift box handcrafted with paint and fabric. Make it as unique as your friend. Change the colors to complement her home and tailor what you put inside to her tastes. It's all about taking the time to say, "Thanks for being my friend."

Materials

1 (10½") heart-shaped papier-mâché box
1 (11") square batting
Fabrics: 1 (19") square and 1 (11") square yellow-and-pink print, 1 (6" x 7") piece yellow, dark pink and green scraps
Aleene's Tacky Glue™
Aleene's Fusible Web™
Black dimensional paint
1"-wide sheer pink ribbon: 1 (34") length, 1 (22") length
Aleene's Premium-Coat™ Acrylic Paints: True Yellow, True Apricot, Medium Fuchsia, True Green, True Fuchsia
Aleene's Premium Designer Brushes™: shader, liner
Fine-tip permanent black marker

Directions

1 Place box lid on batting and trace. Cut out batting heart. Using batting heart as guide, cut 1 heart from 19" print fabric square, adding about 4" all around. With edges aligned, glue batting heart on top of box lid. Let dry. Center lid batting side down on wrong side of fabric heart. Fold and glue excess fabric to inside of box lid. Let dry.

2 Transfer pocket pattern to solid yellow fabric and cut 1. Fuse ½"-wide strips of web to side and bottom edges on wrong side of pocket. Turn under side and bottom edges of pocket along fold lines indicated on pattern and fuse. Fuse 1 (½"-wide) strip of web to top edge on wrong side of pocket. Turn under top edge of pocket and fuse.

3 Fuse web to wrong side of dark pink and green fabric scraps. Cut 3 (1¼"-diameter) circles from dark pink for flowers. Transfer leaf pattern to green and cut 3. Referring to photo, fuse flowers and leaves to pocket. Referring to photo, embellish pocket, flowers, and leaves with dimensional paint. Let dry. Glue pocket onto box lid. Glue 34" ribbon length around sides of box lid. Tie remaining ribbon in bow and glue bow to box lid. Let dry.

4 Paint inside and outside of box True Yellow. Let dry. Lightly brush True Apricot paint over painted surface of box to add shading. Let dry. Referring to photo, paint ½"-diameter Medium Fuchsia circles for flowers and True Green leaves around sides of box at bottom. Let dry. Add shading to each flower with True Fuchsia. Let dry. Draw vine and details on flowers and leaves, using marker. Write "Friendship is truly a treasure to be cherished forever" or desired words around sides of box above painted designs, using marker.

5 Using box as guide, cut 1 heart from remaining print fabric. Glue fabric heart inside box bottom. Let dry.

Write a favorite poem or the words to a favorite song along the sides of your box.

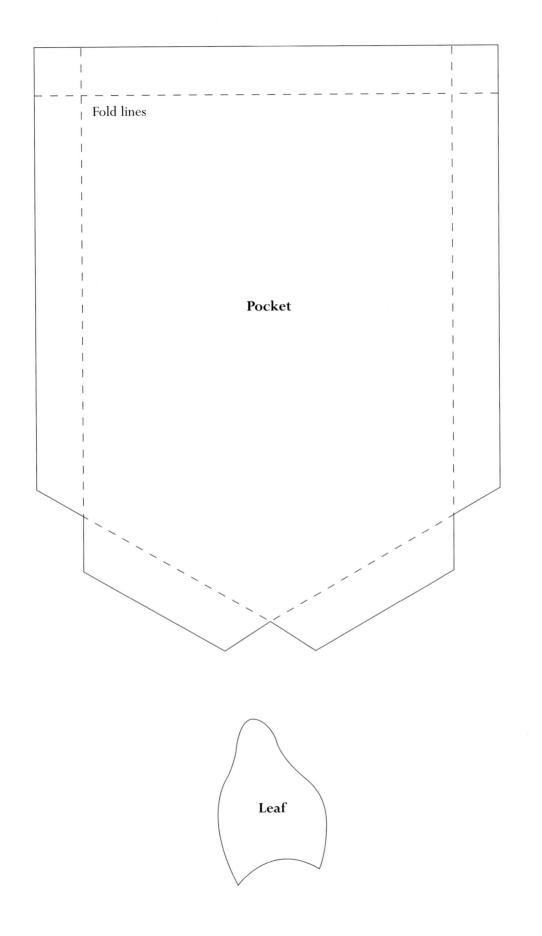

Fold lines

Pocket

Leaf

Bear Hug Cookie Jar

Delight a friend with a jar full of "beary" good cookies. The purchased cookie jar is easy to decorate using the technique described here.

❧ Materials ☙

Aleene's Tissue Paper™: light brown, medium brown, blue gingham, red gingham, ivory gingham
Glass cookie jar
Sponge paintbrush
Aleene's Reverse Collage Glue™
Dimensional paints: black, dark brown, light brown, rust, navy
Aleene's Satin Sheen Twisted Ribbon™: beige

Directions

1 Transfer patterns to tissue paper and cut 1 bear from light brown, 1 of each inner ear and 1 muzzle from medium brown, 1 banner from blue gingham, and 5 hearts from red gingham. Measure height and circumference of jar; add ½" to each measurement. Cut 1 piece of ivory gingham tissue paper to these measurements.

2 Working over small area at a time, brush thin coat of glue onto outside of jar. With 1 long edge of paper aligned with top edge of jar, press ivory gingham paper into glue, pressing out any air bubbles. Wrap paper around jar, overlapping ends ½", and glue excess paper to bottom of jar. Brush top of paper with glue. Let dry.

3 Glue inner ears and muzzle in place on back of bear cutout, using glue sparingly. Referring to photo for positioning, glue tissue-paper cutouts onto jar in following order: banner, bear, and hearts. Brush coat of glue on top of all tissue paper pieces to seal all edges. Let dry.

4 Paint details on tissue paper designs as follows, letting dry between colors. Draw facial features on bear with black paint. Outline muzzle and inner ears with dark brown paint. Outline bear and write "Cookies" on banner with light brown paint. Outline banner and add dots to banner with rust paint. Outline each heart with dots of navy paint.

5 Measure circumference of jar at top; add about 24" to that measurement. Cut 1 length of twisted ribbon to this measurement. Untwist ribbon. Tear ribbon into narrow lengthwise strips. Holding several narrow strips together, tie strips in bow around top of jar.

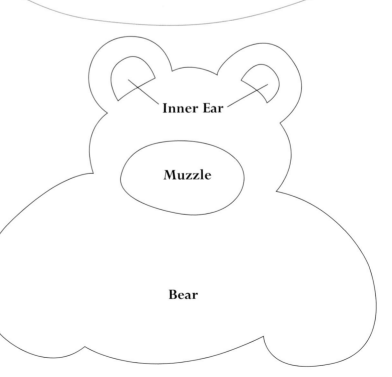

Banner

Heart

Inner Ear

Muzzle

Bear

Bears are one of the most popular and frequently used motifs in home-decor crafting. Fire up your imagination and adapt this bear pattern to other designs. For example, fuse fabric bears onto place mats or napkins or glue a felt bear onto a wreath for your door.

131

Soothing Bath Oils

Pamper your mother or best friend with homemade aromatic bath oils, a fragrant and lovely way to help her relax and unwind.

❧ Materials ❧

For each: Clean, dry bottle with tight-fitting cork stopper or lid
Funnel
2 vitamin-E capsules for each ounce of oil
Paraffin
Assorted ribbons and trims to decorate bottle
Aleene's Designer Tacky Glue™
For tangerine oil: Assorted small yellow and orange dried flowers
Olive oil to fill bottle
5 drops tangerine essential oil for each ounce of olive oil
For lavender oil: Assorted small dried flowers
Olive oil to fill bottle
5 drops lavender essential oil for each ounce of olive oil
For almond-rose oil: Assorted small dried flowers
Almond oil to fill bottle
5 drops rose geranium oil for each ounce of almond oil

Directions

1 **For each,** put flowers in bottle. Fill bottle with olive or almond oil, using funnel. Cut open vitamin-E capsules and squeeze oil into bottle. Add essential oil. Replace cork stopper in bottle.

2 Melt paraffin over low heat. Invert bottle and dip into wax several times, letting each coat dry before dipping again. Glue ribbons and assorted trims to bottle as desired.

Bath-Oil Tips

• When selecting dried flowers to put into bath oil, be sure to purchase flowers that were grown and preserved without pesticides or chemicals. Or gather flowers from your garden and dry them yourself.
• Instead of dried flowers, put dried herbs, seashells, colored pebbles, or glass stones into the oil for decoration.
• Save glass bottles from your recycling bin to use as containers for bath oil. Look for cork stoppers in kitchen shops.
• Let the bath oil mixture stand for about 7 days to allow it to blend thoroughly.
• Store bath oil in a cool, dark place, since heat and sunlight can alter the color and the composition.
• If desired, substitute safflower oil for olive oil or almond oil, or use a mixture of oils to create your own special blend. We do not recommend mineral oil, since it may clog pores.
• Purchase olive oil or safflower oil in a grocery store. You can find almond oil in a health food store or a pharmacy.
• Essential oils are found in some crafts stores or health food stores. To order essential oils by mail, write to The Herbal Sanctuary, 426 Fruit Farm Road, Royersford, PA 19468.

Novel Container Candles

For unique candles, begin with unique bases. Choose containers that fit both the recipient's home decor and personal taste. Add a favorite scent or color to bring pleasure to her day.

❧ Materials ❧

For each: Block of candle wax
Electric skillet
Aluminum foil
Small aluminum loaf pan
Wax dye pellets (optional)
Essential oil (optional)
Candle wicking
Metal wick holders
Mold sealer
Wooden skewers
For seashell candle: Seashell
For flowerpot candle: Small terra-cotta pot
Sheer ribbon (optional)

Directions

1 **For each,** on protected work surface, break wax block into small chunks. Line skillet with aluminum foil and heat to 300°. Place wax chunks into loaf pan. Then put loaf pan into skillet. Slowly melt candle wax. (It takes 20 to 30 minutes.) For colored wax, add dye pellets while melting wax. For scented candles, add essential oil.

2 Thread 1 wick end through wick holder. Using mold sealer, anchor wick holder to bottom of shell or pot. (Make sure to completely fill hole of pot with sealer.) Tie other end of wick to wooden skewer so that skewer rests flush on rim of pot or shell.

3 Slowly pour wax into shell or pot to within ¼" of rim. Wax will shrink from sides of container while it hardens. Add remaining melted wax to fill sides of container. Let harden. Remove skewer and cut wick to within 1" of rim. Cut to ¼" above candle when ready to light.

4 For flowerpot candle, wrap with sheer ribbon, if desired. Remove ribbon before lighting candle.

For a special botanical treat, scent the wax for these potted candles with essential oils in aromas found in your garden.

Rosebud Stationery

Have fun decorating note cards and a matching stationery holder for a lady of letters. Use her favorite colors or copy the colors shown here.

Materials
(for 1 stationery holder, 1 note card and envelope, and 1 letter-paper set)

1 yard Aleene's Fusible Web™
½ yard fabric
Aleene's Box Maker™ and Box Blanks™ (large)
Hot-glue and glue sticks
1 yard flat lace with single-scalloped edge
Aleene's Premium-Coat™ Acrylic Paints: Deep Fuchsia, Medium Fuchsia, Deep Violet, Dusty Violet
Paintbrushes
Dimensional paints: green, pink, light blue, purple, gold
½ yard 1"-wide and ¼ yard ¼"-wide ribbons in desired colors
¼" hole punch
Raffia scrap
1 blank note card with matching envelope
1 (8½" x 11") sheet blank white paper with matching envelope
Decorative-edged scissors
1 (6" x 4½") envelope

Directions for stationery holder

1 Fuse web to wrong side of fabric. Remove paper backing. Fuse fabric to large box blank. Cut fabric-covered blank into 11¼" x 15" rectangle.

2 Along width, mark line through center of blank side of rectangle. Using scoring base and scoring tool from kit, score center line. Measure and mark 2" from 1 long edge of rectangle on blank side. Score marked line. Fold 2" scored edge to blank side of rectangle. Referring to photo, cut V shape in center of 2" edge. Fold along center line. Referring to photo, cut each outside edge of 2" edge at angle. Hot-glue outside edges and V-shaped edges.

3 Cut lace to fit along edges of folder front. Cut fusible web into 4 (½"-wide) strips. Fuse web strips along edges on right side of front cover. Iron lace strips onto fusible web strips.

4 Referring to photo and using Deep Fuchsia and Medium Fuchsia or Deep Violet and Dusty Violet, paint rosebuds on front cover of holder. Let dry. Using dimensional paints, add rosebud leaves, stems, and other floral dots. Let dry.

5 Tie 1"-wide ribbon in bow. Trim edges. Hot-glue bow at top of rosebud stems. Referring to photo, punch holes along back and front cover edges. Tie holder closed with raffia.

Directions for note card and envelope

Using same technique as described in Step 4 of directions for stationery holder, paint front of cards to match motif on front of holder. For bow, follow Step 5 of directions for stationery holder, using ¼"-wide ribbon. Repeat to make multiple cards. Place in stationery folder with matching envelopes.

Directions for letter-paper set

Cut sheet of blank white paper in half widthwise. Trim top edge of paper with decorative-edged scissors. Using same technique as described in Step 4 of directions for stationery holder, paint rosebuds in top left-hand corner of paper. Repeat technique to decorate matching envelope flap. Repeat to make multiple sets. Place sets in stationery folder.

If you cannot find a frilly blank note card, purchase a plain one, cut strips from a paper doily place mat, and glue the lace strips along the edges of the card.

137

Crafting
with Heidi

Heidi finds joy in spending time crafting in her studio each day.

TISSUE PAPER

FLAT LACE

*F*rom gluing tips to fusible web how-tos, Heidi shares her wealth of crafting knowledge in the following pages.

Heidi is thrilled to teach her grandchildren, Savannah and Austin, all about crafts.

Heidi's 8 Great Secrets

1 Tips for Successful Gluing

To make Aleene's Tacky Glue™ or Aleene's Designer Tacky Glue™ even tackier, leave the lid off for about an hour before using it so that excess moisture evaporates.

Too much glue makes items slip around; it does not provide a better bond. To apply a film of glue to a project, make a cardboard squeegee by cutting a 3" square of cardboard (cereal box cardboard works well). Then use this squeegee to smooth the glue onto the craft material.

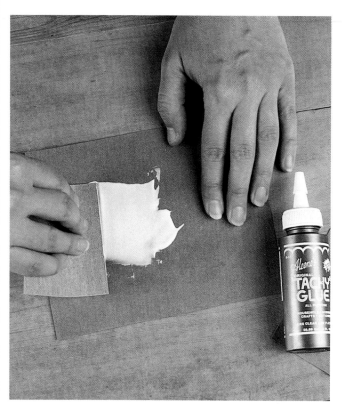

A small piece of cardboard makes a good squeegee.

2 Temporary Tape Tip

To apply consistent fine lines of glue, refer to the diagrams below to make a tape tip for your glue bottle.

1. Using 4"-long piece of transparent tape, align 1 long edge of tape with edge of nozzle. Press tape firmly to nozzle to prevent leaks.

2. Rotate bottle to wrap tape around nozzle. Tape will reverse direction and wind back down toward bottle.

3. Press tail of tape to bottle for easy removal.

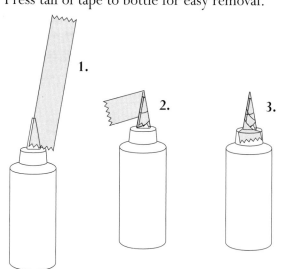

3 Using a Paintbrush for Gluing

Here are a few things to keep in mind when selecting a paintbrush to use with glue. Choose a soft-bristle brush so that you won't tear the paper when you brush on the glue. Be sure the bristles are firmly attached to the brush to prevent them from getting caught in the glue and ending up a part of your craft project. A ½" shader brush is a good size to use for most crafts. Heidi recommends separate paintbrushes for paint and glue. Always wash and dry your brushes immediately after use (before the glue or the paint dries) to prolong their usefulness and to keep them in top condition.

4 Sponge-painting Secrets

"Sponge painting is a quick-and-easy way to apply paint to a craft," says Heidi. "I use a natural sea sponge to get a textured background effect, and I often cut shapes from a pop-up craft sponge to paint a motif on a project." Here are a few hints that will help you become a master at sponge painting.

• Always dampen a natural sea sponge or a pop-up craft sponge with water before dipping the sponge into the paint. Be sure to thoroughly wring out the excess water so you won't dilute the paint.

• After dipping the sponge into the paint, blot the excess paint on a paper towel to keep from applying too much paint at one time.

• If the sponge becomes saturated with paint, rinse it thoroughly in clean water and wring out the excess water.

• To make a pop-up craft sponge shape easier to hold while painting, cut 2 side-by-side slits in the back of the sponge. Each slit should be about ¾" long and ¼" deep. Insert your forefinger and thumb into the slits to get a good grip on the sponge. If your sponge shape is too small for slits, simply pin a large safety pin to the back of the sponge and use it as a handle (see the photo).

Cut slits in the back of a sponge to make it easier to hold.

5 Brush Up on Your Painting Techniques

For each of her painting projects, Heidi uses Aleene's Premium-Coat™ Acrylic Paints because she is able to get the coverage she wants in as few coats as possible.

The perfect companions to Aleene's paints are Aleene's Enhancers™. These enhancers, when used with Aleene's acrylic paints, endow the paint with a variety of capabilities. **Primers,** such as *All-Purpose Primer,* prepare your surface (except fabric) for even coverage of your base coat. Aleene's primer also protects the surface of the item being painted. Because it dries clear, it works well when you want to maintain a natural finish.

Mediums are always mixed with an acrylic paint and are never used alone. Mix *Textile Medium* with acylic paint to make the paint pliable so that it can be absorbed into fabric fibers. No heat setting is required and your fabric will retain its softness. Mix *Clear Gel Medium* with acrylic paint so that the paint can be used as a stain or as an antiquing paint. Mix *Glazing Medium* with acrylic paint to thin the colors for transparent looks. Mix *Mosaic Crackle Medium* with the acrylic paint to create an easy faux finish. Use the Mosaic Crackle Medium in conjunction with *Mosaic Crackle Activator.*

Varnishes ensure your piece will be protected. *Satin Varnish* dries to a soft finish, and *Gloss Varnish* dries to a shiny finish. Both varnishes dry clear.

Although Aleene's paints clean up easily with soap and water, be sure to thoroughly rinse your paintbrushes or sponges immediately after use to prevent the paint from hardening in the bristles or in the sponge.

When stamping or sponge-painting a design, it's a good idea to first practice on a piece of paper to determine the correct placement and proper amount of pressure and paint needed for the desired effect.

Keep in mind that because you trace the shape on the wrong side of the fabric, the appliqué is a mirror image of the pattern when it is fused in place.

6 Working with Aleene's Fusible Web

Use Aleene's Fusible Web™ to create fast and easy no-sew projects. For the best results, always wash and dry fabrics and garments before applying fusible web, in order to remove any sizing. Do not use fabric softener in the washer or the dryer.

Lay the fabric facedown on the ironing surface. (A hard surface, such as a wooden cutting board, will ensure a firm bond.) Lay the fusible web, paper side up, on the fabric. With a hot, dry iron, fuse the web to the fabric by placing and lifting the iron. Do not allow the iron to rest on the web for more than one or two seconds. Do not slide the iron back and forth. Remember, you are only transferring the glue web to the fabric, not completely melting the glue.

Transfer the pattern to the paper side of the web and cut out the pattern as specified in the project

directions. Or referring to the right side of the fabric, cut out the desired portion from a print fabric.

To fuse the appliqué to the project, carefully peel the paper backing from the appliqué, after making sure the web is attached to the fabric. (If the web is still attached to the paper, re-fuse it to the appliqué before fusing the appliqué to the project.) Arrange the appliqué on the desired prewashed fabric or other surface, as listed in the project directions. If you are fusing more than one appliqué, place all the appliqués in the desired positions and then fuse them in place. With a hot, dry iron, fuse the appliqués to the project by placing and lifting the iron. Hold the iron on each area of the appliqués for approximately five seconds.

Applying lines of dimensional paint to the edges of your fused appliqués provides a finished look but is not necessary.

7 Handcrafted Means Hand-Wash

After creating a beautiful wearable, you will want to care for it properly. Be sure to let the glue or the paint on your new garment dry for at least one week before washing. This allows the embellishment to form a strong bond with the fabric. (For glitter designs, wait two weeks before washing.)

Protect your work from the rough-and-tumble treatment of a washing machine. Turn the garment wrong side out, wash by hand, and hang to dry.

8 Embroidery Stitches

To make **blanket** or **buttonhole stitches,** knot one end of your floss. Referring to Diagram A, push the needle up from the wrong side of the fabric, even with the edge of the appliqué. Insert the needle into the appliqué and then come up at the edge again, keeping the floss below the point of the needle. Continue stitching in this manner, keeping your stitches even. The stitches should be approximately ³⁄₁₆" long and ¼" apart.

To make **straight stitches,** knot one end of your floss. Referring to Diagram B, push the needle up from the wrong side of the fabric. Insert the needle up and down in the fabric as shown. Vary stitch lengths as desired.

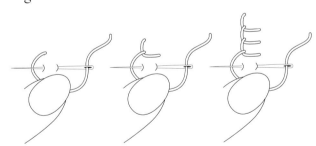

Diagram A: Blanket or Buttonhole Stitches

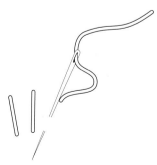

Diagram B: Straight Stitches

Metric Conversion Chart

U.S.	Metric
⅛"	3 mm
¼"	6 mm
⅜"	9 mm
½"	1.3 cm
⅝"	1.6 cm
¾"	1.9 cm
⅞"	2.2 cm
1"	2.5 cm
2"	5.1 cm
3"	7.6 cm
4"	10.2 cm
5"	12.7 cm
6"	15.2 cm
7"	17.8 cm
8"	20.3 cm
9"	22.9 cm
10"	25.4 cm
11"	27.9 cm
12"	30.5 cm
36"	91.5 cm
45"	114.3 cm
60"	152.4 cm
⅛ yard	0.11 m
¼ yard	0.23 m
⅓ yard	0.3 m
⅜ yard	0.34 m
½ yard	0.46 m
⅝ yard	0.57 m
⅔ yard	0.61 m
¾ yard	0.69 m
⅞ yard	0.8 m
1 yard	0.91 m

Index